PAT BROWN, MBA

# Financial Literacy For Widowers

*"Rebuilding Your Financial Life After Loss, One Step at a Time"*

ABRAM 47 BROWN

*First published by AbramBrown47 2025*



*First edition*

*ISBN: 978-1-967737-20-8*

*This book was professionally typeset on Reedsy.*
*Find out more at reedsy.com*

# Contents

# Preface

**Financial Literacy for Widowers**

Losing a spouse changes everything.

In a single moment, life becomes a new, unfamiliar landscape filled with emotional, mental, and financial challenges that few feel prepared to face.

The financial side of loss often arrives with painful urgency. Bills continue to arrive. Paperwork demands attention. Decisions about homes, insurance policies, retirement accounts, and everyday cash flow must be made, even as grief clouds the mind and heart.

For many widowers, stepping into the financial role that a spouse once handled feels overwhelming. Whether you were once deeply involved in the financial decisions or largely left them in your partner's hands, navigating money matters alone can feel like facing a foreign world without a map.

This book was created to offer that map.

It is not meant to be read in one sitting.

It is not intended to overwhelm you with technical jargon or pressure you to make every decision immediately.

Instead, it is designed to meet you wherever you are in your journey — with clarity, compassion, and practical steps you can take at your own pace.

Each chapter focuses on a specific area of your financial life: stabilizing your immediate situation, understanding survivor benefits, managing debts and investments, planning for the future, and rebuilding your sense of security and possibility.

You will find plain explanations, real-world examples, and action steps that respect the emotional realities of grief and the real demands of financial life after loss.

The journey through widowhood is not linear.

Healing takes time.

So does financial rebuilding.

There will be days when you feel strong enough to tackle a major decision, and days when even reading a few pages feels like too much. That is okay.

This book is here whenever you are ready — a steady companion offering guidance, support, and hope.

Financial literacy after loss is not about mastering every detail.

It is about regaining confidence.

It is about protecting what matters most.

It is about honoring your past while building a sustainable, dignified future.

You are not alone in this.

And you do not have to walk this new financial path without a guide.

Welcome to *Financial Literacy for Widowers*.

# Reason for Writing This Book

When I first sat down to imagine this book, I didn't see it as just another financial guide.

I saw faces.

I saw conversations.

I saw moments at kitchen tables, in offices, in quiet phone calls that stretched long into the evening — moments where men who had lost their wives sat across from me, trying to piece together a life they no longer recognized.

I didn't plan on writing a book for widowers.

But life has a way of putting you exactly where you're needed.

Over the years, in my work as a financial advisor and educator, I kept meeting men who were grappling with more than just grief. They were grappling with decisions about mortgages, retirement accounts, insurance claims, taxes, debts, investments — all while carrying a sadness so heavy it showed up in the way they walked, in the way they spoke, in the way they couldn't always finish a sentence without swallowing hard.

I realized that, after the flowers faded and the casseroles stopped coming, what remained was often an enormous pile of financial responsibility — with very little guidance on how to handle it, especially while grieving.

And what made it harder was that many of these men had spent years trusting their wives to manage the household finances, or to share that load equally. Now they were being asked to learn an entire new language while in the middle of heartbreak.

I decided I had to do something.

Not because I had all the answers.

But because I had seen too many good men feel overwhelmed, ashamed, isolated, and scared.

This book was born from a simple desire:

to sit across from you, even if only through these pages, and say,

*"You are not alone. You are not failing. And you can do this."*

It's deeply personal for me, too, because I've seen up close how fragile financial stability can become after loss.

I've witnessed how easy it is to be taken advantage of, how quickly fear can cloud judgment, how paralyzing the smallest financial decisions can feel.

And I know that rebuilding is not just about dollars and cents — it's about dignity, confidence, and hope.

You deserve a financial life that honors the love you shared with your spouse.

You deserve tools, information, and support that feel steady, patient, and real.

You deserve a guide that speaks to your heart as much as your wallet.

That's why I wrote this book.

Not just to teach you about money.

But to walk beside you as you rebuild a life that is still full of meaning, strength, and possibility.

One chapter at a time.

One decision at a time.

One breath at a time.

You're not alone.

And your best days are still ahead.

# Acknowledging the Emotional, Mental, and Financial Toll of Losing a Spouse

There's no easy way to say this:

Losing your spouse changes everything.

Not just emotionally, but mentally, physically, spiritually — and financially.

One moment, you're part of a team.

The next, you're standing alone, looking around at a life that feels completely unfamiliar.

Grief isn't just sadness. It's confusion.

It's waking up and forgetting, for a few seconds, that your world has changed — only to remember all over again.

It's being exhausted but unable to sleep.

It's forgetting simple things — where you put your keys, what you were supposed to do today — because your brain is carrying a load it was never meant to carry alone.

And when it comes to money, that load gets even heavier.

Bills still show up.

Bank accounts still need tending.

Insurance claims, retirement accounts, home maintenance, taxes — none of it pauses for grief.

It all keeps coming, at a time when you have the least energy, the least clarity, and the least emotional capacity to deal with it.

The financial toll is real.

But so is the mental and emotional toll of having to make major life decisions while your heart is still in pieces.

For many widowers, there's also an extra layer of fear:

*"What if I make a mistake?"*

*"What if I lose everything we built together?"*

*"What if I can't do this on my own?"*

If you're feeling that way, please know:

You are not failing.

You are grieving.

And grief makes even the simplest tasks feel monumental.

There is no manual that prepares you for what it feels like to sit down with a stack of paperwork when you would give anything to have your spouse back instead.

There is no quick checklist that can erase the ache in your chest when you have to retitle a bank account or decide what to do with a retirement plan you once thought you'd enjoy together.

This is hard.

It's harder than most people know.

And it's not just about getting through a few tough weeks.

Grief — and financial transition — is often a long, uneven journey.

There will be days when you feel strong enough to tackle paperwork, make a few calls, maybe even feel a small sense of progress.

There will be other days when simply opening the mail feels like too much.

That's okay.

There's no straight line through this.

No "right way" to grieve.

No "perfect" way to rebuild.

There is only your way, your pace, your healing.

This book was written with that reality in mind — with respect for how heavy the emotional, mental, and financial toll truly is.

You won't find pressure here.

You won't find judgment.

You'll find small steps, gentle reminders, clear explanations, and steady encouragement.

Because rebuilding your financial life after losing your spouse isn't just about spreadsheets and bank accounts.

It's about rebuilding trust in yourself.

It's about believing that, even now, you are still capable of making good decisions.

That you can still protect what matters.

That you can still create a life of dignity, security, and peace.

You are carrying a lot.

More than anyone should have to.

And yet, here you are — still moving forward.

That is strength.

You are stronger than you think.

You are braver than you feel.

And you are absolutely capable of reclaiming your financial life, one step at a time.

# You Are Not Alone — And You Can Rebuild

I want you to hear this clearly:

You are not alone.

Even if it feels like the world has moved on and left you behind, you are not the only one walking this difficult road.

There are millions of men who have stood where you're standing now — staring at a life they no longer recognize, trying to figure out what comes next.

Some have felt overwhelmed by paperwork.

Some have felt terrified of making a mistake.

Some have sat at their kitchen tables with unopened envelopes, afraid to even look.

You are not weak for feeling any of those things.

You are human.

You are grieving.

And you are doing the best you can.

The truth is, you don't have to have it all figured out right now.

You don't have to tackle every financial task in a day, or a week, or even a month.

You don't have to be perfect.

You simply have to keep moving — one small step at a time.

Maybe today it's reading a chapter in this book.

Maybe tomorrow it's gathering important documents.

Maybe next week it's setting up an appointment with a financial advisor or calling your bank to retitle an account.

It doesn't have to be fast.

It doesn't have to be flawless.

It just has to keep moving forward — even if some days all you can manage is a half-step.

You can rebuild your financial life.

You can protect your future.

You can create stability and peace for yourself and for the people you love.

It may feel impossible right now.

But the impossible is built one ordinary step at a time.

And you won't have to walk that path alone.

This book is designed to walk with you — page by page, decision by decision, moment by moment.

You are not alone.

You are not failing.

You are rebuilding.

And even in this season of loss, your life, your dignity, your future — they still matter.

You still matter.

# How to Use This Book (Slowly, Chapter by Chapter, When Ready)

This is not the kind of book you are expected to read in one sitting.

This is not a race.

This is not a checklist to power through.

And this is certainly not a test you can pass or fail.

This book is meant to be a **companion** — a steady, patient guide you can turn to when you're ready, at whatever pace makes sense for you.

Some chapters might feel immediately important. You might read one and feel a sense of relief, because it answers a question that's been weighing on you.

Other chapters might feel too heavy to face right now. That's okay.

Skip them for now.

Come back later when you feel stronger or when the time is right.

You don't have to go through this book in perfect order.

You don't have to absorb every detail all at once.

You don't have to understand everything the first time you read it.

You're allowed to read slowly.

You're allowed to pause often.

You're allowed to put the book down for a week and pick it up again when you feel ready.

Every chapter is designed to stand on its own, so you can find the help you need when you need it, without feeling overwhelmed by the rest.

You might come back to the same page two, three, four times.

You might highlight a sentence that brings you comfort.

You might dog-ear a page that answers a hard question.

You might cry while reading.

You might feel a wave of strength when you least expect it.

All of that is normal.

All of that is allowed.

Think of this book like a trusted friend who's willing to sit with you — in silence if needed — and only speak when you're ready to hear the next piece of guidance.

You are in control of how you move through these pages.

You are allowed to make your healing and rebuilding journey your own.

Whenever you're ready — whether today, tomorrow, or months from now — this book will be waiting, right where you left off.

You are not behind.

You are not doing it wrong.

You are simply walking forward, one chapter, one page, one small brave step at a time.

# Why Financial Literacy Matters After Loss

## The Landscape After Loss

When you lose your spouse, life as you knew it ends.

It's not just the loss of the person you loved; it's the loss of routines, dreams, plans, conversations — and very often, the shared responsibility of managing your financial life.

Bills don't pause for grief.

Insurance companies don't send condolence letters instead of paperwork.

Mortgage lenders, banks, and investment accounts don't offer a "healing window" before decisions must be made.

The hard truth is that financial tasks demand your attention almost immediately after loss, even when you feel least capable of facing them.

And that's why financial literacy — real, grounded, practical financial literacy — matters so much in the aftermath of grief.

Because even though you didn't ask for this situation, you now have a new financial life to manage.

And you deserve to manage it with clarity, confidence, and dignity.

## Why It Feels Harder Than Anyone Admits

First, let's name something important:

Handling money after loss isn't just a matter of "getting organized" or "being responsible."

It's much, much deeper than that.

Every financial decision you face — from retitling the house to deciding what to do with a life insurance payout — is tied to the person you lost.

Selling a car isn't just a transaction; it's letting go of memories of road trips and shared errands.

Filing a death certificate isn't just paperwork; it's confronting the finality of loss in black-and-white text.

This emotional weight affects your ability to think clearly.

Grief fog is real.

Decision fatigue is real.

Financial fear is real.

You are not imagining it.

You are not weak.

You are carrying an invisible burden that makes every step harder than it looks on paper.

Acknowledging that is the first step toward approaching your financial life with the patience and compassion you deserve.

## Why Financial Literacy Matters Now More Than Ever

Financial literacy matters after loss because:

- **You are now the primary decision-maker** for your household finances.
- Whether you handled the money before or not, the full weight of financial management now rests on your shoulders. Understanding your options protects you.
- **Mistakes made during grief can have long-term consequences.**

- Rushed decisions about selling a home, cashing out retirement accounts, or choosing investments can haunt you financially for years. Knowledge gives you breathing room.
- **Predators target widowers.**
- Sadly, financial scams targeting grieving spouses are common. Knowing the basics of what's normal — and what's not — helps you spot and avoid exploitation.
- **Financial literacy empowers emotional healing.**
- When your financial house feels even a little more in order, you create space in your mind and heart for actual grief work. One reinforces the other.
- **You are protecting your future self.**
- The decisions you make in the first year after loss can shape your financial security for the next 10, 20, 30 years. Educating yourself is a form of self-respect.

## Common Financial Pitfalls Widowers Face

Let's gently walk through a few of the most common financial traps widowers fall into — not to shame, but to protect:

- **Making Major Decisions Too Quickly**
- Selling the house within weeks. Cashing out retirement plans. Giving away money out of guilt or impulse.
- Grief creates urgency, but most financial decisions benefit from time and space.
- **Trusting the Wrong People**
- Well-meaning (or not-so-well-meaning) acquaintances may push you toward financial products, investments, or legal moves that aren't truly in your best interest.
- **Avoiding All Decisions Indefinitely**
- Grief paralysis can make it tempting to ignore financial tasks altogether. But avoidance usually compounds stress — and sometimes financial

damage — over time.

- **Letting Emotions Drive Spending**
- "Retail therapy" after loss is real. Big purchases to fill the void — cars, vacations, home remodels — can leave you financially vulnerable.
- **Failing to Update Legal and Financial Documents**
- Old beneficiaries, outdated wills, insurance policies in your late spouse's name — these can cause serious complications down the road if not addressed.

Knowing these pitfalls is not about blaming yourself if you recognize some of these patterns.

It's about giving yourself the tools and time to course-correct with grace.

## What Financial Literacy Really Means

Financial literacy doesn't mean memorizing tax codes or becoming a day-trader.

It doesn't mean becoming an overnight expert in insurance, estate planning, or investing.

It means:

- Knowing enough to ask good questions
- Feeling confident enough to say "I don't understand, explain it again"
- Recognizing when a deal seems too good to be true
- Understanding the basic building blocks of your financial life
- Feeling less intimidated when paperwork or decisions arise
- Protecting yourself and your loved ones from unnecessary risk

Financial literacy isn't about perfection.

It's about empowerment.

## Action Steps You Can Take Today

**Step 1: Give yourself permission to learn slowly.**

You are allowed to take your time. You are allowed to reread. You are allowed to ask for help.

**Step 2: Create a "Financial Pause" List.**

Write down any major financial decisions you feel pressured to make.

Then next to each one, write: "Pause. Revisit later."

Give yourself permission to wait 6–12 months on anything that isn't urgent.

**Step 3: Identify Your Trusted Inner Circle.**

This might include a financial advisor, attorney, accountant, or a trusted family member.

Not the loudest voices — the most trustworthy ones.

**Step 4: Start a Financial Journal.**

Keep a simple notebook where you track financial tasks, questions, and reflections.

Grief can cloud short-term memory. Writing things down lightens the load.

**Step 5: Celebrate Small Wins.**

Opened a letter you were afraid to face? Celebrate it.

Made an appointment with a financial advisor? Celebrate it.

Small steps are still steps.

## Tools and Decisions Widowers Commonly Face

Let's break down a few key areas widowers usually navigate:

**Estate Planning Updates**

- Update wills, trusts, and powers of attorney
- Re-title assets and property
- Review and update beneficiary designations

**Social Security Adjustments**

- Apply for survivor benefits
- Understand how your age affects payout amounts
- Consider timing carefully

**Insurance Changes**

- File life insurance claims
- Update or reassess health insurance coverage
- Review long-term care insurance needs

**Investment and Retirement Accounts**

- Understand your options for IRAs, 401(k)s, pensions
- Avoid cashing out accounts unless absolutely necessary
- Reassess risk tolerance after loss

**Debt Management**

- Evaluate outstanding debts in your spouse's name and your own
- Understand how debts transfer (or don't) after death
- Make a plan for high-interest obligations first

**Housing Decisions**

- Decide whether to keep, sell, or rent your home
- Understand financial implications of downsizing or relocating
- Protect yourself from rushing into a sale too quickly

## Real-World Scenario: "Tom's Story"

Tom lost his wife of 38 years unexpectedly.

She had handled most of the finances — paying bills, managing investments, filing taxes.

In the first month after her death, Tom was inundated with paperwork. He felt paralyzed.

A neighbor recommended an advisor who pressured him to invest his insurance payout immediately into an annuity he didn't understand.

Tom almost signed — but something didn't feel right.

He paused.

He reached out to his brother-in-law, who connected him to a fee-only advisor who patiently explained all his options.

Today, Tom's investments are simple, understandable, and aligned with his needs.

He stayed in his home, updated his legal documents, and built a monthly financial checklist that he feels confident managing.

His key lesson?

*"Pause. Ask questions. Trust your gut. Get second opinions."*

You can do the same.

## Reflection: The Heart Behind Financial Literacy

Financial literacy after loss isn't about becoming a spreadsheet wizard.

It's about regaining your agency.

It's about knowing you are still capable of protecting yourself.

It's about honoring the life you shared — by protecting the life you still have left to live.

Grief and financial healing walk side by side.

Some days will feel strong.

Some days will feel like starting over again.

But every small financial step you take is a statement of hope:

*"I'm still here. I'm still building. I'm still honoring my future."*

## In Closing

You are not alone.

You don't have to rush.

You don't have to know everything today.

You can take it step by step.

You can rebuild with dignity and peace.

You can protect what matters most.

Financial literacy after loss is not just about managing money.

It's about believing — in time — that life can still be good.

It's about trusting yourself again, piece by piece.

And it starts right here, right now, with one page, one choice, one small act of courage at a time.

You are doing better than you think.

# Common Mistakes Widowers Make (And How to Avoid Them)

## Introduction: It's Not About Blame — It's About Grace

First, let's get one thing absolutely clear.

This chapter isn't here to shame you.

It's not here to list out ways you've "failed" or "done it wrong."

It's here to wrap an arm around your shoulder and quietly say,

*"Hey, a lot of good men before you made these same mistakes. Let's learn from them, not repeat them."*

Because the truth is, when you're grieving, overwhelmed, scared, and exhausted, **mistakes are easy to make**.

They aren't proof you're irresponsible.

They're proof you're human.

And once you know the most common pitfalls, you can protect yourself — slowly, steadily, wisely — from making choices today that you might regret tomorrow.

Let's walk through them together.

## Mistake #1: Making Big Financial Decisions Too Quickly

When you're grieving, you just want the pain to stop.

You want to simplify your life.

You want to *do something* to regain a sense of control.

This often shows up as **rushing into big financial decisions** like:

- Selling the house immediately
- Cashing out retirement accounts
- Buying a new car, RV, or boat
- Moving across the country
- Giving large sums of money to family or charity without a plan

You might feel an intense pressure to *change everything* right away.

You might think:

*"If I can just start over somewhere else, this hurt will ease."*

But here's the reality:

**Grief clouds judgment.**

And decisions made under intense emotion are rarely the right ones long-term.

**Pros of waiting:**

- Gives your emotions time to settle
- Allows you to make decisions with your long-term future in mind, not just your current pain
- Prevents costly financial mistakes that are hard to reverse

**Cons of rushing:**

- Selling a home and regretting it later
- Incurring huge taxes or penalties for cashing out investments early
- Spending money on purchases that feel good temporarily but hurt your financial security long-term

**Action Step:**

Make a "One-Year Rule" for yourself:

*No major financial moves for 12 months unless absolutely necessary.*

## Mistake #2: Trusting the Wrong People

In the months after loss, it can feel like everyone has an opinion about what you should do with your money.

Some people mean well.

Others, frankly, don't.

Widowers are often targeted by:

- Aggressive insurance salespeople
- Investment brokers pushing high-commission products
- Family members subtly (or not so subtly) angling for gifts, loans, or inheritance

It's not always easy to tell who has your best interests at heart.

Especially when you're lonely, vulnerable, and craving connection.

**Pros of pausing before trusting:**

- Gives you time to vet advisors properly
- Helps you separate sincere advice from self-serving pitches

**Cons of trusting too quickly:**

- Ending up locked into unsuitable financial products
- Losing money to scams or poor advice
- Creating strained family relationships

**Action Step:**

Before making any financial move based on someone else's recommendation, ask:

*"Is this person financially benefiting from my decision?"*

If the answer is yes — pause, get a second opinion.

## Mistake #3: Ignoring Paperwork and Financial Maintenance

It's understandable:

Paperwork feels overwhelming.

Dealing with account transfers, title changes, insurance claims — it all feels like an avalanche when you're barely staying upright emotionally.

But ignoring it doesn't make it go away.

In fact, it often makes things harder later.

Examples of paperwork that needs timely attention:

- Retitling bank accounts and property
- Updating beneficiaries on retirement accounts and life insurance
- Filing insurance claims
- Paying outstanding bills or debts

**Pros of facing paperwork:**

- Preserves your legal and financial rights
- Reduces future complications for you and your heirs
- Gives you a growing sense of control and accomplishment

**Cons of avoiding paperwork:**

- Missed deadlines (which could mean losing benefits)
- Unclaimed assets
- Legal battles down the road

**Action Step:**

Create a "**Financial Paperwork Checklist**" and tackle one item per week.

Small bites make a big difference.

## Mistake #4: Overspending as a Form of Comfort

Loss leaves a void.

And sometimes, spending money can feel like filling that void — temporarily.

Common grief-driven spending patterns:

- Expensive vacations
- Home renovations
- Luxury items (cars, watches, jewelry)
- Lavish gifts to children or grandchildren
- Hobby overindulgence (golf trips, new collections, etc.)

There's nothing wrong with wanting comfort.

But when comfort spending threatens your long-term security, it becomes a second source of pain.

**Pros of budgeting for small comforts:**

- Allows space for joy without sacrificing stability
- Helps you feel rewarded without regret

**Cons of unchecked grief spending:**

- Drains savings faster than planned
- Creates guilt or financial stress later
- Can mask, but not heal, emotional wounds

**Action Step:**

Set up a "**Joy Budget**" — a specific dollar amount you can use for comfort spending each month without guilt.

## Mistake #5: Forgetting to Update Estate Planning

After your spouse dies, your estate plan doesn't automatically update itself. It must be reviewed and changed — ideally with an attorney's help. Key items to revisit:

- Your will
- Power of attorney documents
- Healthcare directives
- Trusts
- Beneficiary designations

If you don't update these, assets might go to the wrong people, or your wishes might not be carried out the way you intend.

**Pros of updating:**

- Protects your heirs and your wishes
- Reduces court involvement later
- Gives you peace of mind

**Cons of postponing:**

- Your old estate plan could cause legal chaos
- Strangers (not family) might make critical decisions for you
- Taxes and fees could increase unnecessarily

**Action Step:**
Schedule a meeting with an estate planning attorney within six months of your spouse's passing.

## Mistake #6: Overestimating or Underestimating Retirement Needs

After a spouse dies, your financial situation changes — sometimes dramatically.

- Your expenses may go down in some areas (like healthcare premiums if one spouse was older)
- Your income may also drop (loss of Social Security benefits, pension reductions, etc.)

Without clear retirement planning, widowers often:

- Overestimate how much they have and overspend
- Underestimate how long they'll live and under-save

**Pros of revisiting your retirement plan:**

- Provides clarity about what you can realistically afford
- Helps you adjust your lifestyle without fear

**Cons of ignoring it:**

- Risk of running out of money later
- Forced lifestyle reductions when you least expect them

**Action Step:**
Work with a financial advisor to create a **Widower-Specific Retirement Projection** — based on your new life realities.

## Mistake #7: Avoiding Professional Help Out of Fear or Pride

Some widowers think they have to figure it all out alone.

Maybe it's pride.

Maybe it's fear of being sold something.

Maybe it's just not wanting to face it yet.

But going it alone can be dangerous, especially if you're not used to managing all aspects of finances yourself.

**Pros of seeking professional help:**

- Access to specialized knowledge
- Emotional support during big decisions
- Protection from costly mistakes

**Cons of going it alone:**

- Risk of oversight
- Greater vulnerability to scams
- Missing opportunities for growth and security

**Action Step:**

Interview at least three professionals (advisors, CPAs, estate attorneys) — not to hire immediately, but to practice building a team you can trust.

## Real-World Scenario: "Robert's Story"

Robert lost his wife of 44 years.

Overwhelmed, he immediately sold their family home, cashed out a pension, and gave large financial gifts to his grandchildren.

He thought he was "doing the right thing" — starting fresh.

But two years later, Robert realized he didn't have enough to sustain his lifestyle.

His generosity and fast moves cost him his own security.

If Robert could rewind time, he says he would have waited a full year, sought professional advice, and created a written financial plan before making any big decisions.

You can learn from Robert's hard-earned wisdom — without living through the same regret.

## Encouragement: Mistakes Are Part of the Journey

If you've already made one of these mistakes — breathe.

You are not doomed.

You are not ruined.

You are not a failure.

You are grieving.

You are learning.

You are doing the best you can with the information and energy you have.

And every day is a fresh chance to make a new decision — a stronger, wiser one.

## Closing Reflection

Financial literacy after loss is not about achieving perfection.

It's about finding clarity in a season of chaos.

It's about protecting yourself with knowledge, compassion, and patience.

It's about honoring your future without rushing your grief.

You are not alone.

You are not behind.

You are rebuilding — one step at a time.

And your future, even now, is still filled with hope, possibility, and peace.

# "First, Breathe." — Immediate vs. Non-Immediate Financial Decisions

## Starting Where You Are

If you're holding this book right now, chances are your world has been turned completely upside down.

You may not know which end is up.

You may not remember if you ate breakfast today.

You may feel like you're carrying an invisible weight around your chest every minute of every day.

And now — somehow — you're supposed to figure out paperwork, bills, accounts, taxes, insurance, investments, real estate, and legal documents?

It's too much.

So before we talk about finances, I want you to do one thing.

**Breathe.**

Right here.

Right now.

Breathe.

Not a quick, shallow gasp — a real breath.

In through your nose.

Out through your mouth.

Slow it down.

Feel your chest rise and fall.

You are here.

You are alive.

And you are doing the best you can.

There is no prize for rushing through grief.

There is no award for making the fastest decisions.

The best financial move you can make in the early days is often simply **to pause**.

To breathe.

To allow yourself space.

Because not every decision needs to be made right now.

Some things can — and should — wait.

## Understanding the Two Kinds of Financial Decisions

After loss, you'll face two broad categories of financial decisions:

**Immediate decisions** — things that require action within days or weeks

**Non-immediate decisions** — things that can wait months, sometimes even a year or more

The problem is, when you're grieving, it's hard to tell which is which.

Everything feels urgent.

Everything feels important.

Everything feels overwhelming.

So let's slow it all down.

Let's sort it out — together.

## Immediate Financial Decisions (The Ones You Should Prioritize)

There are a few things that do require fairly quick action after your spouse passes away.

Not everything, but a few critical areas.

Here's a breakdown:

### *1. Obtaining Death Certificates*

You'll need multiple certified copies of your spouse's death certificate — usually between 10 and 20 copies.

Why?

Because almost every institution — banks, insurance companies, government agencies — will ask for an official copy.

**Action Step:**

Order extra copies through the funeral home or directly from the county.

### *2. Notifying Key Institutions*

Certain organizations need to know about the death promptly:

- Social Security Administration (to stop benefits or initiate survivor benefits)
- Life insurance companies (to start claims)
- Employer HR departments (if your spouse was still working)
- Banks and investment firms (to begin retitling accounts)

**Action Step:**

Create a list of institutions to notify, and work through them slowly — not all in one day.

### *3. Securing Immediate Income*

If you relied on your spouse's income, you'll need to figure out:

- Survivor Social Security benefits
- Pension survivor benefits
- Life insurance payouts
- Short-term access to savings or joint accounts

**Action Step:**

Meet with your bank or financial advisor to identify available funds for the next 6-12 months.

### *4. Protecting Accounts and Assets*

Sadly, identity theft can happen after someone passes away.

Protect yourself by:

- Closing credit cards held solely in your spouse's name
- Freezing your spouse's credit reports with the three major bureaus
- Monitoring your own accounts carefully for suspicious activity

**Action Step:**

Set up fraud alerts and keep copies of all closure letters for your records.

### *5. Paying Critical Bills*

Some bills cannot be ignored, even during grief:

- Mortgage or rent
- Utilities
- Health insurance premiums
- Minimum debt payments

**Action Step:**

Set up automatic payments if possible to avoid missed due dates while you're in the fog of grief.

## Non-Immediate Financial Decisions (The Ones You Should Pause)

Most financial decisions **do not need to be made immediately.**

In fact, making them too soon can cause regret, financial loss, and unnecessary heartache.

Here are major areas where **waiting is often the best financial move**:

### *1. Selling Your Home*

You may feel tempted to sell the house right away — to escape the memories, to downsize, to simplify.

But real estate decisions made during grief are often regretted later.

Give yourself at least 12 months if possible before deciding.

**Pros of Waiting:**

- Allows emotional attachment to fade before making a financial choice
- Provides time to assess whether moving is truly necessary
- Avoids impulsive pricing or timing mistakes

**Cons of Rushing:**

- Possible underpricing
- Moving costs you hadn't factored in
- New housing may not be right for your long-term needs

### *2. Making Major Purchases*

After loss, it's common to feel impulsive — to buy a new car, a new home, a vacation package — anything to feel better.

Large purchases right after loss are often a way to try to soothe grief.

Give yourself a "waiting period" — 3 to 6 months minimum — before any major financial commitment.

**Pros of Waiting:**

- Gives you clarity on what you truly want and need
- Protects your retirement savings
- Reduces the chance of buyer's remorse

### *3. Changing Investment Strategies*

You might feel a sudden urge to change everything about your investments.

Maybe you feel the need to "get aggressive" to make up for lost income.

Maybe you want to "pull everything out" to keep it safe.

Neither extreme is usually wise.

**Action Step:**

Work with a fiduciary financial advisor who can help assess your risk tolerance post-loss without rushing you into radical changes.

### *4. Gifting or Loaning Money to Family*

This is a big one.

After loss, many widowers feel pressure — spoken or unspoken — to help adult children, grandkids, or relatives financially.

Before you start giving large gifts or co-signing loans, make sure your own financial house is fully secure first.

**Action Step:**

Set personal financial boundaries before offering financial help to others.

### *5. Remarrying and Financial Entanglements*

Some widowers find love again quickly — and that can be a beautiful thing.

But blending finances with a new partner requires **extreme caution**.

You'll need to update estate plans, prenups, beneficiary designations, and more.

**Action Step:**

Move slowly with financial merging — protect yourself and your heirs.

## Real World Scenario: "Joe's Story"

Joe lost his wife suddenly after 32 years of marriage.

Within six months, he sold their home, moved three states away, gave each of his kids $50,000, and bought a sports car he'd always dreamed of.

By the end of the first year, Joe realized:

- He hated his new city
- He missed his old friends
- His savings had taken a major hit
- The excitement of the sports car wore off quickly

If Joe could go back, he says he would have waited at least a full year before making **any major changes**.

Your story doesn't have to follow the same path.

## A Breathing Room Plan

Here's a simple plan you can follow:

1. **Immediate Decisions:**

- Death certificates
- Notify institutions
- Secure income
- Protect accounts
- Pay critical bills

1. **Pause for 12 Months on:**

- Selling the house

- Major purchases
- Investment strategy changes
- Financial gifts or loans
- Remarriage and financial merging

## Reflection: Permission to Pause

Grief already feels like drowning.

You don't have to make it worse by forcing yourself into decisions you're not ready to make.

You are allowed — **encouraged** — to take your time.

To breathe.

To listen to your intuition.

To honor the life you shared by protecting the life you still have.

## Closing Encouragement

You are doing better than you think.

Every breath you take, every small financial task you complete, every time you choose to pause instead of rush —

you are reclaiming your life.

Grief is not a straight line.

Financial healing is not a checklist.

Both journeys happen in fits and starts, in moments of courage and moments of rest.

Breathe.

Move slowly.

And trust:

your future is worth the careful rebuilding you're doing today.

# The Financial Rebuilding Timeline Overview: What Happens in the First Month, Six Months, and Year

## Introduction: Building Through the Storm

If you're reading this, I want you to know something right away.

You are doing better than you think.

It might not feel like it.

You might feel like you're barely holding things together.

You might feel like every task is an uphill climb in a rainstorm.

But the very fact that you're willing to look ahead — even just a little bit — shows strength, even if you can't feel it yet.

Grieving the loss of your spouse while trying to rebuild your financial life is not easy.

It's messy, uneven, exhausting work.

And no one hands you a roadmap.

This chapter is meant to change that.

I want to give you a timeline — not a rigid schedule, but a **steady, flexible framework** — for what financial rebuilding looks like after loss.

So you can know what to expect.

So you can pace yourself.

So you can take things one step at a time.

Not everything must be done today.

Not everything must be figured out tomorrow.

Grief is not a straight line.

Neither is financial rebuilding.

But with patience, knowledge, and steady movement, you will rebuild — stronger, wiser, and freer.

Let's walk through it together.

## Part 1: The First Month – Stabilizing and Securing

The first month after losing your spouse is often a fog.

Nothing feels real.

You are operating on instinct, running on fumes, and trying to simply make it through the next hour.

The financial goal for the first month is **stabilization**, not perfection.

You are not expected to have a full financial plan yet.

You are simply securing the basics.

Here's what matters most during the first month:

### *Immediate Action Steps*

**1. Order Multiple Death Certificates**

You'll need 10–20 certified copies.

They are required for banks, Social Security, insurance, and legal matters.

**2. Notify Key Institutions**

Social Security Administration, banks, investment firms, insurance companies, your spouse's employer (if applicable).

**3. Secure Immediate Income**

File for survivor Social Security benefits, if eligible.

File life insurance claims if applicable.

Access joint accounts if needed.

**4. Protect Against Identity Theft**

Close your spouse's credit cards.

Freeze their credit reports.

Monitor your own credit closely.

**5. Keep Critical Bills Paid**

Mortgage or rent.

Utilities.

Health insurance.

Minimum debt payments.

### *Emotional Reminders*

- You do not need to make any major financial decisions yet.
- You are allowed to move slowly.
- You are allowed to grieve and still be strong.

## Part 2: The First Three Months – Organizing and Understanding

As the initial shock begins to ease slightly (and it may take longer — everyone's timeline is different), you will slowly begin to shift into the **organization phase**.

Think of this period as clearing the ground before rebuilding.

### *Core Priorities*

**1. Gather and Organize Financial Documents**

Bank statements, insurance policies, investment accounts, retirement plans, wills, trusts.

**2. Take Inventory of Assets and Debts**

List everything you own (assets) and everything you owe (debts).

**3. Create a Temporary Budget**

Estimate what your income and expenses look like now.

This is not your forever budget — just a rough working version.

**4. Review Health Insurance Coverage**

Make sure your own coverage is active and appropriate.

**5. Schedule an Estate Planning Review**

If you had a will or trust with your spouse, it likely needs updating.

**6. Create a Calendar for Important Deadlines**

Tax filing dates, insurance renewals, bill due dates, estate settlement timelines.

### *Emotional Reminders*

- You are allowed to cry while filling out forms.
- You are allowed to ask for help from professionals.
- You are allowed to take breaks and come back to tasks later.

## Part 3: The First Six Months – Evaluating and Planning

At around the six-month mark, you may begin to feel a subtle shift.

The sharpest edges of grief might still be there, but you might also find small pockets of clarity.

This is the time to **evaluate** — not rush — the bigger pieces of your financial picture.

### *Key Areas to Address*

**1. Retirement Planning Reevaluation**

Your retirement strategy may need major adjustments.

Meet with a trusted financial advisor to reassess based on:

- Your new income sources
- Your new living expenses
- Updated goals

**2. Investment Portfolio Review**

Avoid gut-driven moves like selling everything or swinging to risky investments.

Instead, calmly realign your investments with your updated time horizon and risk tolerance.

**3. Housing Decisions (but only if truly necessary)**

If staying in your current home is financially sustainable and emotionally bearable, staying put often brings stability.

If not, this is a good time to **start** researching — **not rushing** — potential moves.

**4. Debt Management Plan**

If you carry credit card debt, loans, or a mortgage, create a clear plan for managing or reducing it sensibly.

**5. Long-Term Insurance Needs**

Evaluate if you still need life insurance, disability insurance, or long-term care insurance now.

**6. Begin Updating Beneficiaries**

On all IRAs, 401(k)s, life insurance policies, and financial accounts.

### *Emotional Reminders*

- Feeling tired doesn't mean you're doing it wrong.
- Small steps still count.
- You are building a strong foundation, one piece at a time.

## Part 4: The First Year – Rebuilding and Redefining

The one-year mark is a major milestone.

It doesn't mean the grief is "over."

It doesn't mean you'll have all the answers.

But it often means you are ready to shift from **reacting** to **rebuilding**.

This is where real financial clarity starts taking root.

### *Big Picture Goals*

**1. Create a Comprehensive New Financial Plan**

With help from a financial planner if possible.

Include:

- Income streams
- Spending plan
- Savings goals
- Retirement projections
- Investment strategy
- Insurance coverage
- Estate plan updates

**2. Update or Create a New Will and Estate Plan**

This ensures your assets will be handled according to your wishes.

**3. Set New Financial Goals**

You get to dream again.

Travel, hobbies, family support, charitable giving, a new home — these are not selfish; they are part of living.

**4. Revisit Housing if Needed**

If downsizing or relocating still feels right after a year, move thoughtfully, with a full plan.

**5. Explore Giving Back**

Some widowers find healing in setting up scholarships, foundations, or other charitable endeavors in honor of their spouse.

### *Emotional Reminders*

- Redefining your life is not a betrayal of your spouse's memory.
- Building a stable financial future honors the love you shared.
- You are allowed to feel joy, peace, and hope again — and still miss them.

## Real-World Example: "David's Year of Rebuilding"

David lost his wife of 40 years.

In the first month, he barely paid the bills.

By month three, he had organized their financial paperwork with the help of his daughter.

By month six, he met with a financial advisor and made a new retirement plan.

By the one-year mark, David had downsized to a smaller home near his grandchildren and created a small memorial fund at his church in his wife's honor.

None of it was rushed.

None of it was easy.

But each small step, taken with patience, built a strong new foundation.

You can do the same.

## Quick Reference Timeline

**First Month:**

- Stabilize income and bills
- Protect accounts
- Notify key institutions

**First Three Months:**

- Organize documents
- Build a temporary budget
- Inventory assets and debts

**First Six Months:**

- Reassess retirement and investments

- Evaluate insurance needs
- Start gentle housing considerations

**First Year:**

- Build a full financial plan
- Update estate documents
- Set new financial and life goals

## Closing Encouragement: Your Future Is Still Worth Building

You didn't choose this path.

You didn't ask for this rebuilding project.

But here you are — brave enough to face it anyway.

You are allowed to grieve and rebuild at the same time.

You are allowed to feel lost and still find your way forward.

Financial stability after loss is not just about dollars and cents.

It's about honoring the love you shared — by protecting the life you are still blessed to live.

Take it one breath at a time.

One day at a time.

One small decision at a time.

You are rebuilding not just a financial life —

but a future filled with meaning, strength, dignity, and hope.

# Part 1 Stabilizing Your Immediate Financial Life

The days and weeks after losing your spouse are a whirlwind of emotions, responsibilities, and unexpected decisions.

You are grieving, overwhelmed, and possibly facing financial tasks that feel foreign or unbearable.

This part of the journey is not about having all the answers — it's about **steadying the ship** so you can keep moving through the storm.

**Part 1: Stabilizing Your Immediate Financial Life** is focused entirely on **small, necessary, manageable steps** that bring order to chaos.

We are not building the whole future yet.

We are not solving every financial problem yet.

We are simply securing what needs to be secured right now — calmly, patiently, and one step at a time.

In this section, you'll learn:

- **What financial tasks truly matter immediately**, and what can wait
- **How to prioritize the essentials** like accessing income, paying critical bills, and protecting your accounts
- **How to organize paperwork and financial information** without feeling overwhelmed
- **How to gently create breathing room** between grief and financial

decisions

You'll also discover real-world examples of widowers who took small actions — even through the fog of grief — and how those steps gave them strength for the road ahead.

Each chapter in Part 1 is structured to help you:

- Focus only on what absolutely must be done in the first month or two
- Pause and breathe between tasks, without guilt
- Build the foundation you will need for later financial decisions

You will not be asked to rush.

You will not be asked to make major life decisions while your heart is still in pieces.

Instead, you will be given **clarity**, **calm**, and **compassion** —

the tools you need to **stabilize your financial life one small decision at a time**, while honoring your grief and protecting your future.

# Chapter 1: What to Do First Financially (The First 30 Days)

## Starting Where You Are

If you're reading this chapter, I want to begin by telling you:

You are doing better than you think.

You might not feel strong right now.

You might feel like you're just surviving minute by minute, drowning in paperwork, bills, emotions, and exhaustion.

You didn't choose this road.

But here you are — and already, by picking up this book, you've chosen to move forward, even if it's just one slow, shaky step at a time.

This chapter is about helping you **stabilize your immediate financial life** in the first 30 days after your spouse's passing.

Not to fix everything.

Not to rush you.

But to gently guide you through the handful of things that actually matter right now.

Let's walk together through the steps.

## Step 1: Secure Important Documents

The first step in stabilizing your finances after loss is **securing the paperwork** that forms the backbone of your financial life.

In the fog of grief, it's easy to misplace documents or forget which ones you even need.

But having these in one place will make everything else that follows a little easier.

**Key Documents to Gather:**

- Certified copies of your spouse's death certificate (order 10–20)
- Marriage certificate
- Your spouse's Social Security card (if you have it)
- Life insurance policies
- Wills and trusts
- Titles to property (house, vehicles, etc.)
- Recent bank and investment account statements
- Recent credit card statements
- Loan documents (mortgage, auto loans, personal loans)
- Last two years of tax returns
- Retirement account documents (IRAs, 401(k)s, pensions)

**Why It Matters:**

You will need these documents for everything from filing insurance claims to retitling assets to applying for survivor benefits.

**Action Step:**

Set up a folder — physical, digital, or both — and label it "Critical Financial Documents."

Each time you complete a task and use one of these documents, file it right back.

When the fog rolls in (and it will), you'll be grateful you know exactly where to look.

## Step 2: Freeze Unnecessary Automatic Payments (Temporarily)

Right now, money might be flowing out of your accounts without you even realizing it.

Automatic payments — for subscriptions, memberships, services — could continue draining your cash flow at a time when every dollar matters.

**Examples of Things to Freeze or Review:**

- Streaming services
- Gym memberships
- Subscription boxes
- Club memberships
- Automatic charitable donations

You're not deciding forever today.

You're just temporarily pausing **anything nonessential** until you have a clear financial picture.

**Why It Matters:**

During grief, it's hard to track money.

Stopping the slow leaks now gives you breathing room to plan later.

**Action Step:**

Print your last 60 days of bank and credit card statements.

Highlight every automatic payment.

Make a quick decision: keep, freeze, or cancel.

Freezing for now is not failure.

It's smart triage.

## Step 3: Notify Key Institutions

Certain institutions need to be formally notified of your spouse's death.

This isn't just paperwork — it's critical to protecting your finances and ensuring you receive the benefits you're entitled to.

**Key Institutions to Notify:**

- **Social Security Administration** — to stop any ongoing benefits and apply for survivor benefits
- **Banks and Credit Unions** — to secure accounts and retitle joint accounts
- **Life Insurance Companies** — to begin claim processes
- **Employer HR Departments** — if your spouse was still employed, you may be entitled to final paychecks, benefits, or pensions
- **Investment Firms** — for accounts that need retitling or transfer
- **Mortgage Lenders** — if your spouse was on the mortgage

**Why It Matters:**

Unnotified institutions can continue pulling money from accounts, issue tax documents incorrectly, or leave benefits unclaimed.

**Action Step:**

Create a simple checklist of institutions and start making calls.

You don't have to finish all at once.

Set a goal: one call per day if that's all you can manage.

Slow progress is still progress.

## Step 4: Access Joint Accounts and Estate Documents

If you shared financial accounts, you'll need to access and retitle them appropriately.

**Common Accounts to Address:**

- Checking and savings accounts
- Retirement accounts (IRAs, 401(k)s)
- Investment brokerage accounts
- Real estate titles
- Vehicle titles

If your spouse had a will or trust, now is the time to review those documents — ideally with the help of an estate attorney — to understand what assets pass directly and what assets require probate.

**Why It Matters:**

Until accounts are retitled or properly transferred, you could face frozen assets, limited access to funds, or legal complications.

**Action Step:**

Meet with your bank's estate department or your financial advisor to start the process of retitling accounts.

Ask clear questions.

Take notes.

You don't have to know everything — you just have to keep showing up.

## Step 5: Immediate Cash Flow Check

Cash flow is your lifeline during grief.

You need to know:

- What money is still coming in (survivor benefits, savings, employment income)
- What money is still going out (mortgage, utilities, insurance, debt payments)

You are not building a perfect budget right now.

You are simply ensuring that **you can cover the essentials** in the next 30, 60, and 90 days.

**How to Do a Basic Cash Flow Check:**

**1. List All Sources of Income:**

Survivor benefits, Social Security, insurance payouts, personal income, savings withdrawals.

**2. List Essential Expenses:**

Housing, utilities, insurance premiums, basic food, transportation.

**3. Identify Gaps or Surpluses:**

If income exceeds essentials, you have breathing room.

If expenses exceed income, you need a temporary plan — maybe cutting discretionary spending or accessing emergency savings.

**Why It Matters:**

Without a basic cash flow check, it's easy to slip into debt or miss critical bills during grief.

**Action Step:**

Create a simple two-column list:

**Income** on one side, **Essentials** on the other.

See the reality clearly — even if it's uncomfortable.

Clarity is the first step to taking back control.

## Real-World Example: "Frank's First 30 Days"

Frank lost his wife, Susan, after 37 years together.

In the first month, Frank could barely get out of bed, let alone face their finances.

But with the help of his daughter, he took small steps:

- Secured all critical documents in a single folder
- Froze three subscription services they no longer needed
- Contacted Social Security and started survivor benefits
- Retitled their joint savings account in his name
- Built a rough cash flow chart on a yellow legal pad

By day 30, Frank still felt deep grief — but also a small, steady sense of strength.

Each completed task became a brick in the foundation he was rebuilding.

You can feel that strength too.

## Closing Reflection: You Are Already Building

The first 30 days after losing your spouse aren't about solving everything.

They're about breathing.

Stabilizing.

Protecting what matters.

You are allowed to move slowly.

You are allowed to take breaks.

You are allowed to feel like you're fumbling your way through.

And yet —

every call you make, every form you fill out, every bill you pay —

is an act of profound courage.

You are not alone.

You are not behind.

You are rebuilding your life, piece by piece, with strength you might not even recognize yet.

Breathe.

Move at your own pace.

And trust that each small step you take is planting seeds for a life that still holds meaning, purpose, and peace.

## Securing Important Documents (Expanded)

You might feel too exhausted to hunt for papers.

That's normal.

But one of the kindest things you can do for yourself right now is to gather **critical documents** — not because you're eager to deal with them, but because it saves you pain later.

### *How to Organize Without Overwhelm:*

**Start with Three Simple Folders:**

- **Folder 1: Legal and Identity Documents**
- (Death certificates, Social Security cards, marriage certificate, will, trust documents)
- **Folder 2: Financial Assets and Debts**
- (Bank accounts, investment statements, insurance policies, mortgages, credit card balances)
- **Folder 3: Income and Tax Documents**
- (Pay stubs, pension documents, Social Security correspondence, tax returns)

**Tip:**

Use an accordion folder, a cardboard box, or a single desk drawer.
It doesn't have to look pretty.
It just has to be accessible.

**Emotional Reminder:**

You're not just gathering paper.
You're protecting your future.

## Freezing or Reviewing Automatic Payments (Expanded)

Automatic payments can be lifesavers when set up intentionally.

But after loss, many of them are leftovers — tied to a life that no longer fits.

### *Questions to Ask About Every Auto-Payment:*

- Does this subscription still serve me?
- Did my spouse primarily use this service?
- Will canceling this help me preserve cash for essentials?

- Could this be paused temporarily without harm?

**Common Auto-Payments Worth Reviewing:**

- Gym memberships (especially family memberships)
- Streaming services (Netflix, Hulu, Amazon, etc.)
- Online storage subscriptions (Dropbox, iCloud upgrades)
- Home maintenance services (lawn care, pest control, cleaning services)

*Pros of Freezing Payments:*

- Frees up immediate cash
- Reduces mental clutter
- Gives you a clean slate to re-evaluate expenses later

*Cons of Canceling Too Quickly:*

- Accidentally canceling necessary services (like utilities bundled with autopay discounts)
- Losing grandfathered-in pricing

**Action Step:**

For anything uncertain, freeze first, cancel later.

Preservation over perfection.

## Notifying Key Institutions (Expanded)

This step feels emotionally brutal — having to say the words "my spouse has passed" over and over again.

Take your time.

Rest between calls if needed.

*Suggested Order of Notification:*

1. **Social Security Administration**
2. (So survivor benefits can be activated and to avoid overpayments.)
3. **Banks and Credit Unions**
4. (Freeze, close, or retitle accounts appropriately.)
5. **Insurance Companies**
6. (Life, auto, home — policies may need updating immediately.)
7. **Investment and Retirement Firms**
8. (Access to IRAs, 401(k)s, and pensions may involve timelines.)
9. **Mortgage Lenders and Creditors**
10. (So they know who is now responsible — you may qualify for hardship options.)

**Tip:**

Prepare a simple script:

*"My name is [Your Name]. I'm calling to report the passing of my spouse, [Spouse's Name]. What steps do I need to take to update or close our accounts?"*

**Emotional Reminder:**

You are not being "dramatic."

You are honoring your loved one — and protecting yourself.

## Accessing and Organizing Accounts (Expanded)

When you open financial portals after your spouse's death, it can feel like opening doors to rooms you didn't know existed.

Go slowly.

Don't panic if you find forgotten accounts, small debts, or investments you didn't know about.

This is normal.

*Common Account Issues Widowers Discover:*

- Old credit cards with zero balances
- Dormant savings accounts
- Forgotten IRAs from previous employers
- Mortgage payments made from joint accounts
- Automatic bill pays tied to a now-frozen bank account

**Tools That Help:**

- A simple spreadsheet
- Password manager apps (for organizing logins securely)
- A trusted family member or advisor to help double-check paperwork

**Pros of Accessing and Retitling Early:**

- Reduces fraud risk
- Clarifies your true financial picture
- Enables smoother transition of assets

**Cons of Delaying Too Long:**

- Institutions may restrict access
- Probate court processes may become more complicated
- Survivor benefits could be delayed

**Action Step:**

Start with accounts that impact your daily cash flow first — checking, savings, utilities — before moving to long-term assets.

## Conducting an Immediate Cash Flow Check (Expanded)

Money feels different after loss.

It often feels smaller.

Scarier.

Slipperier.

And that's exactly why doing a basic cash flow check early on is one of the bravest financial steps you can take.

**You are not budgeting for your future yet.**

You are budgeting for your **next 30 to 90 days**.

### *Focus On:*

- Mortgage/rent
- Utilities (electricity, water, gas, internet)
- Health insurance premiums
- Food (groceries, not restaurants)
- Transportation (gas, car insurance, basic maintenance)

**Temporary Reductions Are Okay:**

- Entertainment expenses
- Dining out
- Travel
- Non-essential shopping

You can bring these back later.

Right now, the goal is **stability**.

### *Real-World Cash Flow Example: "Anna's First Month"*

Anna's income from Social Security survivor benefits and part-time consulting work was about $3,500 per month.

Her necessary expenses — mortgage, food, utilities, car payment, insurance — totaled $2,900.

Her first simple budget gave her breathing room: about $600/month to rebuild savings slowly.

Small surplus, but a **huge emotional victory**.

**Action Step:**

Do your own rough cash flow calculation — even if it's messy.

Knowing is always better than guessing.

### Reflection: Why Small Steps Matter

You might feel like you're moving in slow motion.

That's not weakness.

That's survival.

Every time you gather a document, make a call, freeze a payment, or check a balance — you are planting a flag in the ground that says:

*"I'm still here. I'm still standing. I'm still protecting my future."*

You are doing sacred work.

You are not just managing money.

You are honoring a life you built with your spouse — and protecting the life you are still blessed to live.

## First 30 Days Financial Checklist for Widowers

**In the First 7 Days:**

- Order 10–20 certified copies of the death certificate.
- Notify Social Security Administration.

- Notify your spouse's employer (if applicable).
- Identify all joint bank accounts and important financial documents.
- Set up a simple folder or file system for critical papers.

**By the End of Week 2:**

- Contact life insurance companies to begin claims.
- Freeze any unnecessary automatic payments (subscriptions, memberships).
- Secure immediate cash flow (identify available funds for 1–3 months of bills).
- Protect against identity theft (notify credit bureaus, close cards solely in spouse's name).
- Pay critical bills (mortgage/rent, utilities, minimum debt payments).

**By the End of Week 3:**

- Begin building a simple cash flow chart (income vs. essentials).
- Review health insurance coverage to ensure it's still active.
- Notify investment firms and begin the process of retitling accounts.
- Organize a list of debts (mortgage, credit cards, personal loans) for review.

**By the End of Week 4:**

- Set up a temporary 90-day financial survival budget (nothing fancy — clarity first).
- Contact a trusted estate attorney to discuss wills, trusts, and probate (if applicable).
- Make a master list of accounts, passwords, and financial contacts.
- Give yourself permission to **pause** before making any major financial decisions.
- Celebrate your first month of progress — no matter how small it feels.

## 30-Day Financial Calendar Template for Widowers

**Week 1: "Gather and Notify"**

- Order death certificates.
- Notify Social Security and employer.
- Gather legal, financial, and insurance documents.

**Week 2: "Secure and Protect"**

- Freeze unnecessary payments.
- Protect spouse's identity.
- Pay only critical bills.
- Confirm immediate cash availability.

**Week 3: "Organize and Simplify"**

- Create a basic income/expense tracker.
- Begin list of debts and recurring bills.
- Notify banks and investment firms for account changes.

**Week 4: "Review and Reflect"**

- Build a temporary 90-day spending plan.
- Schedule an estate planning consultation.
- Reflect: What's one thing that made you feel stronger this month?

## Permission Letter to Yourself (for Widowers)

**Permission Letter: Financial Healing After Loss**

Dear [Your Name],

Today, I give myself permission to move slowly.

To not have all the answers.

To grieve and rebuild at my own pace.

To honor my spouse by protecting the life we built — and by protecting the life I still have.

I give myself permission to:

- Ask for help when I need it.
- Say "not yet" to major financial decisions until I am ready.
- Feel overwhelmed some days — and proud of myself other days.
- Cry while paying bills, if that's what healing looks like.
- Celebrate small victories, like making a phone call or filling out a form.
- Protect my financial future without feeling guilty about surviving.

I give myself permission to pause.

I give myself permission to heal.

I give myself permission to hope again.

I am not behind.

I am not failing.

I am rebuilding.

And every small financial step I take today is an act of love — for the life we shared, and for the life that still lies ahead of me.

I am strong enough to do this.

One day at a time.

One breath at a time.

Signed,

[Your Name]

# Chapter 2: Understanding the Estate Process

## Introduction: The Road You Didn't Ask to Walk

You didn't plan to become an expert in estates.

You didn't sign up for legal jargon, endless paperwork, or complicated decisions.

All you wanted was more time with the person you loved.

And yet here you are — handed folders, legal documents, and responsibilities that feel overwhelming when you're still just trying to get out of bed in the morning.

First: **breathe.**

You are not expected to master this overnight.

You are not expected to do it perfectly.

You are only asked to move forward — one small, steady step at a time.

This chapter is here to explain, in simple language, **what the estate process is**,

**what you need to know**,

**what can wait**,

**what needs your attention**,

and most importantly: **how to protect yourself without losing yourself.**

Let's start by breaking down the biggest and most confusing concept first.

## Probate vs. Non-Probate Assets

When someone passes away, everything they owned has to somehow move to a new owner.

Some assets move **through probate,**

and some **bypass probate** completely.

Understanding the difference is key to knowing what you need to handle — and when.

### *What Is Probate?*

**Probate** is the formal legal process where a court oversees the distribution of a deceased person's estate.

During probate, the court:

- Validates the will (if there is one)
- Appoints an executor or personal representative
- Identifies assets
- Pays debts and taxes
- Distributes what's left to the heirs

**Think of probate as a courtroom process for settling an estate.**

It involves paperwork, timelines, and sometimes significant expenses.

### *What Is a Non-Probate Asset?*

**Non-probate assets** are assets that **pass directly** to a beneficiary without needing to go through the court.

These assets were set up in advance to move automatically after death.

**Examples of non-probate assets:**

- Life insurance proceeds with a named beneficiary
- Retirement accounts like IRAs and 401(k)s with a beneficiary
- Bank accounts with "Payable on Death" (POD) designations
- Jointly owned real estate with rights of survivorship
- Trust-owned assets

These assets skip probate because **the instructions for who gets them are already built into the account itself.**

### *Why This Matters to You*

Knowing which assets are probate and which are non-probate determines:

- How much paperwork you'll face
- How quickly you can access money
- How much it will cost to settle the estate
- How much stress (or relief) you'll experience

**Action Step:**

Make a list of major assets and categorize them:
Is it a probate asset or a non-probate asset?
If you don't know yet — that's okay.
Gather the account names and numbers.
A good estate attorney can help you sort it out without pressure.

## Wills, Trusts, and What They Mean for You

The second big piece to understand is what legal documents your spouse left behind — or didn't leave behind.

Let's break it down simply.

### *What a Will Does*

A **will** is a written document that says:

- Who should receive assets
- Who should be the executor (the person handling the estate)
- What final wishes need to be honored (like funeral arrangements)

**Important:**
Having a will doesn't avoid probate.
It simply tells the probate court what your spouse wanted to happen.

### *What a Trust Does*

A **trust** is a separate legal entity that owns assets for beneficiaries.
Trusts can:

- Distribute assets faster and privately (outside of probate)
- Protect assets from creditors
- Manage assets for minors or special needs dependents
- Set rules about when and how beneficiaries inherit

If your spouse set up a trust, the trustee (possibly you) is responsible for managing it according to the trust's rules.

### *What If There's No Will?*

If your spouse died without a will (this is called **intestate**), state law decides who inherits — not you, not your spouse's wishes.
In most states, intestacy laws prioritize:

- Spouse first
- Then children

- Then other relatives (siblings, parents)

**Action Step:**

Locate the most recent will and/or trust.

If you can't find them, contact the attorney your spouse may have worked with.

If there's no document, you'll follow your state's intestacy process.

## Executors, Attorneys, and Your Role

If you're named **executor** (also called personal representative in some states), you are the quarterback of the estate process.

It sounds intimidating — but let's break it down into manageable pieces.

### *What the Executor Does*

The executor's job is to:

- Locate and manage the deceased's assets
- File necessary documents with the court
- Pay valid debts and final taxes
- Distribute assets to heirs according to the will (or state law if no will)

### *Pros and Cons of Being the Executor*

**Pros:**

- You control the pace of the estate process
- You help honor your spouse's wishes
- You maintain some privacy and protection over the process

**Cons:**

- It can be time-consuming (6 months to 2 years depending on complexity)
- Legal responsibility falls on your shoulders
- Family disputes can sometimes flare up

### *Should You Hire an Attorney?*

Often, yes.

Even if you think the estate is simple, an experienced probate attorney can:

- Save you months (or years) of confusion
- Help you avoid costly mistakes
- Protect you legally from missteps

**Action Step:**

Interview 2–3 estate attorneys.

Find one who explains things clearly without talking down to you.

Hiring the right help is not weakness.

It's wisdom.

## Timeline of Settling an Estate

Every estate is different.

But most follow a basic rhythm.

### *The Typical Timeline:*

**Month 1–3:**

- Funeral arrangements and death certificates
- Notify Social Security, banks, insurers
- Locate will/trust

- Start identifying assets and debts

**Month 3–6:**

- Open probate (if needed)
- File initial paperwork with the court
- Secure property and accounts
- Start paying necessary bills (mortgage, insurance)

**Month 6–12:**

- Inventory all assets formally
- Pay outstanding debts and taxes
- Begin liquidating or transferring assets
- Update personal financial plans based on new reality

**Month 12–24:**

- Distribute remaining assets
- Close probate
- Retitle real estate
- Close accounts
- Finalize all paperwork

## *Real-World Example: "Tom's Estate Timeline"*

Tom lost his wife, Mary.
She left a simple will and they had joint bank accounts.
He still needed:

- 6 months to open probate
- 8 months to settle outstanding credit card bills
- 14 months to close the estate formally

Even "simple" estates take time.

Be patient with the process — and with yourself.

## Reflection: You Are Already Doing the Hardest Work

Facing estate tasks after the death of your spouse is one of the hardest, loneliest jobs there is.

Most people never understand the emotional weight behind the paperwork.

But I want you to know:

Every phone call you make, every form you fill out, every document you organize —

it's not just paperwork.

It's love.

It's stewardship.

It's courage.

You are honoring the life you built together — even while building your new life piece by piece.

# Simple Estate Process Checklist for Widowers

**First 30 Days:**

- Order 10–20 certified copies of your spouse's death certificate.
- Locate the most recent will and/or trust documents.
- Notify Social Security Administration.
- Notify banks, credit unions, and insurance companies.
- Secure all financial accounts and freeze any questionable activity.
- Make a list of assets (house, bank accounts, cars, retirement accounts).
- Make a list of outstanding debts (mortgage, credit cards, loans).

**First 90 Days:**

- Consult with an estate attorney (even if the estate seems simple).
- Open probate (if necessary) through the local court system.
- File the will with the court (if required in your state).
- Identify and organize monthly bills to continue paying essentials (mortgage, utilities, insurance).
- Begin inventory of estate assets (valuations, appraisals if needed).

**Months 3–6:**

- Maintain property and safeguard physical assets (home, vehicles).
- Pay valid debts and final expenses from estate funds.
- File final income taxes and, if needed, estate tax returns.
- Start liquidating or transferring assets according to the will or trust instructions.

**Months 6–12:**

- Distribute assets to heirs once debts and taxes are resolved.
- Retitle real estate, vehicles, and bank accounts into your name or beneficiaries' names.
- Close unnecessary accounts and credit cards in your spouse's name.
- Finalize closing the probate process (if applicable).

**Ongoing:**

- Review and update your own estate plan (will, trust, powers of attorney).
- Update all beneficiaries on your retirement accounts, insurance, and financial assets.
- Meet with a financial advisor to build a new long-term financial plan based on your new circumstances.
- Give yourself permission to move at your own pace — healing and rebuilding take time.

## Quick Reference Chart: Probate vs Non-Probate Assets

**Probate Assets Non-Probate Assets**

Property owned solely by your spouse

Life insurance policies with named beneficiaries

Bank accounts in your spouse's name only

Retirement accounts (IRA, 401(k)) with designated beneficiaries

Vehicles titled only in your spouse's name (unless titled jointly)

Bank accounts with "Payable on Death" (POD) designations

Personal belongings and valuables (unless held in a trust)

Property held jointly with "Right of Survivorship"

Investment accounts without beneficiaries

Assets owned by a living trust

**Key Points:**

- **Probate Assets** must go through court to be officially transferred.
- **Non-Probate Assets** pass directly to the named beneficiaries and skip court.

**Action Step:**

When in doubt, check how the asset is titled or designated — and ask an estate attorney for guidance.

## Pause and Reflect Journal Page

*(After Chapter 2: Understanding the Estate Process)*

**Pause and Reflect: Your Estate Process Journey**

Take a quiet moment for yourself.

You don't have to solve everything today.

You don't have to finish every task this week.

You are allowed to move slowly, breathe deeply, and reflect honestly.

Answer these questions in your own time, in your own words:

**1. What financial tasks have I completed so far?**

(List anything — even small wins, like finding the will or calling Social Security.)

**2. What tasks still feel overwhelming or unclear?**

(Write them down — naming them can take away some of their power.)

**3. Who are two people or professionals I can reach out to for help if I feel stuck?**

(Think: an estate attorney, a financial advisor, a trusted family member.)

**4. What emotions have come up for me during this process?**

(There's no wrong answer — grief, anger, exhaustion, fear, even pride.)

**5. What is one small act of self-kindness I can give myself this week?**

(A walk, a phone call with a friend, a break from paperwork.)

**Reminder to Myself:**

*I am allowed to move at my own pace.*

*I am not behind.*

*I am not alone.*

*I am stronger than I feel.*

## Gentle Sample Letter/Email Template for Widowers

*(For notifying Social Security, banks, insurance companies, and other institutions.)*

**Subject Line:**

Notification of Passing: [Spouse's Full Name]

**Dear [Institution's Name or Department],**

My name is [Your Full Name].

I am writing to inform you that my spouse, [Spouse's Full Name], passed away on [Date of Passing].

I would like to understand the next steps regarding [brief description: account closure, benefit transition, insurance claim, etc.].

Here is the information you may need:

- Full name of deceased: [Spouse's Full Name]
- Date of birth: [Spouse's Date of Birth]
- Date of passing: [Date of Passing]
- Account or policy number (if known): [Number]

Please let me know what documentation you require (such as a death certificate or legal forms) and what actions are needed on my part to move forward.

You may reach me at [Your Phone Number] or [Your Email Address] if you need any additional information.

Thank you for your support and understanding during this time.

Sincerely,

[Your Full Name]

[Your Mailing Address]

[Your Phone Number]

[Your Email Address]

**Tip for Widowers:**

- Save a copy of each letter or email you send.
- Keep a simple checklist of who you've notified and when.
- It's okay to send short, factual notes — you don't have to explain your grief or emotions to businesses.

## Simple Printable Estate Progress Tracker

*(For Widowers)*

**Estate Progress Tracker: Step-by-Step**

Use this tracker to gently monitor your progress through the estate process.

There is no race.

There is no "behind."

Just steady, honest movement forward.

Check off each task when completed:

### *Gather Documents*

- Death certificates ordered (10–20 copies)
- Marriage certificate located
- Will or trust located
- Recent bank and investment statements gathered
- Life insurance policies found
- Property titles and deeds located
- Recent tax returns collected

### *Notifications Sent*

- Social Security Administration contacted
- Life insurance companies notified
- Banks and credit unions notified
- Mortgage lender contacted
- Investment firms contacted
- Credit card companies contacted
- Employer (if applicable) contacted for final pay and benefits

### *Accounts and Assets Secured*

- Joint accounts retitled or secured
- Credit cards in spouse's name closed
- Bank accounts reviewed for automatic payments
- Property secured and insured (home, vehicles)

### *Estate Legal Process Started*

- Probate opened (if required)
- Executor appointed (if you are not already named)
- Estate attorney consulted
- Assets inventoried

- Outstanding debts identified and organized

### *Financial Health Check*

- Immediate cash flow reviewed
- Temporary 90-day budget built
- Surplus or shortfall identified
- Professional support team (attorney, CPA, advisor) identified

### *Ongoing and Final Steps*

- Final debts and taxes paid
- Assets distributed according to will or trust
- Remaining accounts closed
- Real estate retitled
- Final court filings made (closing probate, if needed)

**Final Reminder:**

Check off progress **even if it's slow.**

Each completed step is a brick in the strong foundation you are building.

## Short Gentle Checklist: When to Ask for Professional Help

*(Estate Attorney, CPA, Financial Advisor)*

**You Do Not Have to Do This Alone.**

There are moments in the estate process when bringing in a professional is not just wise — it's an act of self-protection and peace of mind.

If any of the following feel true for you, it's time to reach out for help:

**Legal Help (Estate Attorney)**

- You cannot locate a will or trust.
- The will is being contested by family members.
- The estate involves property in multiple states.
- You're unsure whether probate is required.
- Creditors are contacting you aggressively about debts.
- You need help understanding your role as executor or trustee.

**Tax Help (CPA or Tax Advisor)**

- You must file final income tax returns for your spouse.
- The estate might owe estate taxes (typically on large estates).
- You are unsure how survivor benefits affect your taxes.
- You are selling real estate or assets and unsure about tax consequences.

**Financial Planning Help (Financial Advisor)**

- You are unsure how to reinvest life insurance proceeds or inherited assets.
- You want to create a new retirement plan based on your changed circumstances.
- You need help creating a stable monthly budget moving forward.
- You feel overwhelmed managing multiple investment accounts.

- You want a clear, step-by-step financial roadmap for your next chapter.

**Bonus Tip:**

When interviewing professionals, look for those who listen patiently, explain in plain language, and respect your emotional journey — not just your paperwork.

You are hiring them to support you, not to rush or pressure you.

**Closing Reminder:**

Asking for professional help is not weakness.

It is strength.

It is wisdom.

It is protecting the life you still have left to build — one decision, one trusted relationship at a time.

## Healing Wins Journal Page

*(For Widowers — Track Emotional and Financial Victories)*

## Healing Wins: A Journal for Small but Mighty Victories

When you are grieving, it's easy to overlook how far you've come.

Healing doesn't happen all at once.

It happens in tiny, brave moments.

Use this page to track both emotional and financial wins — no matter how small they seem.

Each "win" is a statement:

*"I am still here. I am still rebuilding."*

Write down anything that felt like a victory — whether it was making a phone call, organizing a document, paying a bill, or simply getting through a hard day.

## This Week's Healing Wins:

- I made one financial decision I had been putting off:
- I faced a task that scared me and completed it:
- I asked for help when I needed it:
- I allowed myself to rest without guilt:
- I remembered that grief and healing are not a race:
- I honored my spouse's memory by protecting our life's work:
- I celebrated one small thing that made me smile:
- I took a step toward my own financial future:

**Reminder:**

No win is too small to matter.

Every act of courage — no matter how invisible it seems to the outside world — is a powerful part of your healing story.

Keep moving.

Keep breathing.

You are doing better than you know.

# Sample Financial Organizer Worksheet

*(For Widowers — Starting the Financial Rebuild)*

# Financial Organizer Worksheet: Building Your New Foundation

This organizer is not about overwhelming you.

It's about giving you a clear, steady place to start as you rebuild your financial life — piece by piece, page by page.

You do not need to fill this out in one sitting.

Work through it slowly, patiently, one section at a time.

## Personal Information

- Full Name: ___________________________________________
- Current Mailing Address: ______________________________
- Phone Number: ________________________________________
- Email Address: ________________________________________

## Key Contacts

- Estate Attorney: _______________________________________
- Financial Advisor: _____________________________________
- CPA/Tax Professional: __________________________________
- Trusted Family Member or Friend: ________________________

## Income Sources

- Survivor Social Security Benefits: $__________________
- Pension (if applicable): $__________________
- Employment Income: $__________________
- Investment Income: $__________________
- Other Income (annuities, royalties, rentals): $__________________

## Monthly Essential Expenses

- Mortgage/Rent: $__________________
- Utilities (electric, gas, water, internet): $__________________
- Food/Groceries: $__________________
- Health Insurance Premiums: $__________________
- Transportation (car payment, insurance, gas): $__________________
- Minimum Debt Payments (credit cards, loans): $__________________

## Assets

- Checking Accounts: ________________________________________
- Savings Accounts: __________________________________________
- Investment Accounts (IRAs, 401(k)s, brokerage): ________________
- Real Estate Owned: ________________________________________
- Vehicles Owned: ___________________________________________
- Life Insurance Proceeds: ___________________________________

## Debts

- Mortgage Balance: $____________________
- Auto Loans: $____________________
- Credit Cards: $____________________
- Other Personal Loans: $____________________

## Immediate Financial To-Do List

- Review all sources of monthly income.
- Build a simple cash flow snapshot.
- Secure all major financial accounts.
- Retitle necessary assets into my name.
- Update or create my own estate plan.

**Closing Reminder:**

You are allowed to rebuild slowly.

You are allowed to pause and breathe often.

You are allowed to protect your peace while you protect your financial future.

Your story didn't end with loss.

A new chapter is waiting — and you are strong enough to build it.

## Sample Gentle Monthly Financial Calendar (First Year After Loss)

### Month 1: Stabilize and Breathe

- Secure death certificates.
- Notify Social Security, banks, and insurance companies.
- Freeze unnecessary automatic payments.
- Pay only essential bills.
- Begin simple cash flow tracking.
- Rest often — grief is heavy work.

### Month 2: Organize and Protect

- Gather important legal and financial documents.
- Review and secure bank and investment accounts.
- Start list of assets and debts.
- Schedule a brief consultation with an estate attorney.
- Set one small financial goal: ex. update one account title.

### Month 3: Understand and Clarify

- Begin opening probate (if necessary).
- Review health insurance coverage.
- Begin listing monthly recurring expenses clearly.
- Identify gaps or surpluses in cash flow.
- Celebrate completing one difficult task — even if small.

### Month 4: Strengthen and Simplify

- Retitle property and joint accounts into your name.
- Confirm outstanding debts and make a plan to address them.
- Review survivor benefits and long-term income streams.

- Pause and acknowledge how far you've come emotionally.

## Month 5: Reassess and Realign

- Consult with a financial advisor (fee-only preferred) to check retirement strategies.
- Start a simple savings or emergency fund if possible.
- Revisit temporary spending adjustments.
- Take one financial action that feels empowering (like opening a high-yield savings account).

## Month 6: Review and Reflect

- Check progress on estate settlement process.
- Review outstanding estate bills or tax filings.
- Reflect: What financial lessons have you learned so far?
- Plan one "reward" or rest day for yourself.

## Month 7: Update and Build

- Update beneficiaries on your accounts and insurance policies.
- Revisit your personal estate plan (new will, powers of attorney).
- Identify any outdated documents and update as needed.

## Month 8: Grow Your Knowledge

- Learn basic investing principles if you feel ready.
- Attend a free financial education webinar or workshop.
- Start a small journal noting what financial topics you want to learn more about.

## Month 9: Deepen Support Systems

- Strengthen professional relationships (advisor, CPA, attorney).
- Consider gently connecting with other widowers if you feel isolated.
- Allow yourself space for new dreams — even if they feel scary.

## Month 10: Plan Thoughtfully

- Start planning financially for the next 12 months.
- Build a realistic, flexible monthly budget based on your new lifestyle.
- Begin considering longer-term goals: travel, moving, giving, new hobbies.

## Month 11: Review and Adjust

- Reassess insurance needs: health, auto, life, home.
- Evaluate investment performance or savings strategy if applicable.
- Check on estate finalization progress and remaining to-do's.

## Month 12: Honor and Hope

- Finalize estate closure paperwork if possible.
- Reflect: What did I survive this year that I never thought I could?
- Set one new personal and financial goal for the year ahead.
- Know you are stronger, wiser, and more capable than you ever believed.

## 20 Gentle Financial Affirmations for Widowers

## Gentle Financial Affirmations

You can repeat these aloud, write them in a journal, or simply sit with one phrase on hard days.

You are building emotional strength alongside financial strength.

1. I am doing the best I can, and that is enough.
2. Every small step I take strengthens my future.
3. I honor my spouse's memory by protecting our legacy.
4. I allow myself to heal and rebuild at my own pace.
5. Financial knowledge is a gift I am giving to my future self.
6. I am capable of managing my finances with wisdom and patience.
7. I forgive myself for what I didn't know before.
8. I ask for help when I need it, and I accept support with grace.
9. I am stronger than today's challenges.
10. I deserve peace, stability, and financial security.
11. Grief and healing can exist alongside financial growth.
12. I am creating a life that honors both love and resilience.
13. I protect my energy, my heart, and my financial future.
14. I choose to face my finances with courage, not fear.
15. I am allowed to move slowly; progress is not a race.
16. I celebrate every financial victory, no matter how small.
17. My story is still being written, and brighter chapters are ahead.
18. I invest not just in money — but in my well-being and freedom.
19. I trust myself to make wise, compassionate choices.
20. I am still here. I am still building. I am still enough.

## Sample "Letter to My Future Self"

*(After the First Year of Financial Healing and Grieving)*

## Letter to My Future Self

*(You can read this now. You can write your own version later.*

*You can tuck it away and open it whenever you need a reminder of how far you've come.)*

Dear Future Me,

You have survived what once felt unsurvivable.

You faced the paperwork, the decisions, the loneliness, the fear — and you kept moving.

You didn't have to be perfect.

You just had to keep showing up.

And you did.

You learned that strength doesn't always look like bold action — sometimes it looks like filling out one form while crying, making one phone call through shaking hands, or simply breathing through another hard day.

You learned that grief and rebuilding walk side by side — neither rushing the other, neither canceling the other out.

You took care of the life you shared with your spouse.

You honored their memory by protecting the foundation you built together.

You honored yourself by beginning to dream again.

You now know:

- You are capable of handling your finances wisely and patiently.
- You are allowed to build a life that is both beautiful and different than before.
- You are allowed to hope, to smile, and to love — even through the missing.
- You are still writing your story — and the best chapters are still ahead.

If today is a hard day, that's okay.

You have been through worse, and you have risen.

You are resilient, resourceful, and real.

You are not starting over empty.

You are starting over full — full of love, full of lessons, full of strength you never wanted but now possess.

I am proud of you.

Keep going.

With gratitude and faith,

[Your Name]

# Chapter 3: Social Security and Survivor Benefits

## Introduction: Learning While You're Healing

When you lose your spouse, no one hands you a roadmap.

No one sits you down and says,

*"Here's exactly what you need to do to protect yourself financially."*

You're left trying to rebuild a life while paperwork piles up, bills arrive, and fears creep in.

One of the most important pieces of your financial foundation after loss may come from a place you hardly thought about before: **Social Security survivor benefits**.

This chapter is about slowing things down.

It's about understanding what you're entitled to, how to access it, and what choices you have — without being rushed, pressured, or overwhelmed.

You're not expected to become an expert overnight.

You are only asked to take one step at a time.

Let's start with the basics.

## How Survivor Benefits Work

Social Security is not just a retirement system.

It also includes protections for families who lose a breadwinner.

When your spouse passes away, you may be eligible for monthly survivor benefits based on their work history.

These benefits are designed to **help you financially** while you adjust to your new life.

### *Who Qualifies for Survivor Benefits?*

You may qualify if:

- You were legally married to your spouse at the time of their death.
- Your spouse had enough work credits under Social Security (usually about 10 years of work).
- You meet the age or disability requirements.

Even if you were separated but still legally married, you could be eligible.

If you were divorced but married for at least 10 years, you might also qualify (under certain rules).

### *Important Basics About Survivor Benefits*

- You can start collecting survivor benefits as early as **age 60** (or 50 if you are disabled).
- If you claim benefits before your **Full Retirement Age (FRA)**, your monthly payment is permanently reduced.
- Survivor benefits are based on what your spouse was entitled to — not on what you personally earned.
- You may have the option to switch between your survivor benefit and your own retirement benefit later.

### *Why It Matters for Widowers*

You might not have been the primary financial manager in your household.

Or maybe you handled the day-to-day finances, but never planned for the loss of income that happens after losing a spouse.

Survivor benefits can provide a critical bridge.

They can give you breathing room while you grieve.

They can give you steady income while you rebuild.

They are **yours by right** — because your spouse earned them for you.

**Action Step:**

If you have not seen your spouse's Social Security earnings history, you can request it through SSA.gov or by visiting your local Social Security office.

## How to Apply for Widow(er) Benefits

Survivor benefits are not automatically given.

You must apply.

Here's how to move through the process without adding unnecessary stress.

### *Step 1: Contact the Social Security Administration*

You cannot apply for survivor benefits online.

You must either:

- Call SSA at 1-800-772-1213 to schedule an interview, or
- Visit your local SSA office in person

### *Step 2: Gather the Documents You'll Need*

Before your appointment, try to gather:

- Certified copy of your spouse's death certificate
- Marriage certificate
- Your spouse's Social Security number
- Your Social Security number
- Birth certificates for you and any dependent children
- Your spouse's most recent tax returns or W-2s (optional but helpful)

Don't worry if you can't find everything perfectly.
Bring what you have.
SSA can often help fill in gaps.

### *Step 3: Attend the Interview*

Your appointment might be in-person or over the phone.
They'll walk you through:

- Your eligibility
- Your monthly benefit options
- When you can start
- Whether it makes sense to take benefits now or wait

You are allowed — and encouraged — to ask questions.
This is your financial security.
You deserve clear answers.
**Timing Tip:**
Apply for survivor benefits **as soon as possible** after your spouse's passing.
Retroactive benefits are limited, usually to six months.
Delaying could mean losing out on important months of income.

**Action Step:**

Make the appointment early, even if you don't feel ready to make decisions.

Starting the conversation is progress.

## Claiming Rules Based on Your Age and Your Spouse's Work History

Social Security survivor benefits depend heavily on two things:

- **Your age** at the time of application
- **Your spouse's earnings record**

Here's what that means for you.

### *If You Are 60 or Older*

You can claim survivor benefits starting at age 60.

However:

- If you claim before your **Full Retirement Age (FRA)** (between 66 and 67 depending on your birth year), your monthly amount will be permanently reduced.
- If you wait until your FRA, you receive **100%** of the benefit your spouse was entitled to.

**Example:**

If your spouse was entitled to $2,000/month at full retirement, and you claim at 60, you might only receive about $1,430/month permanently.

### *If You Are 50–59 and Disabled*

If you have a disability that started before or within 7 years of your spouse's death, you can apply for **disabled widow(er) benefits** starting at age 50.

This benefit requires you to pass Social Security's medical disability requirements — which is a separate process from just being widowed.

### *If You Are Caring for Young or Disabled Children*

If you are caring for your spouse's child who is:

- Under age 16, or
- Disabled

You may be able to collect **survivor benefits at any age**, even if you're younger than 60.

Once the child turns 16 (unless disabled), your caregiver benefits generally end.

### *Important Note About Your Own Retirement Benefit*

If you qualify for your own Social Security retirement benefit later:

- You can start with survivor benefits first
- Then switch to your own higher retirement benefit later (or vice versa)

Social Security will explain your options when you apply.

**Action Step:**

When you meet with SSA, ask them to run scenarios:

"What happens if I take survivor benefits now versus later?"

Knowledge = power.

## Special Situations to Know About

Not every situation fits neatly into the rules.
Here are some special cases widowers should know about.

### *Special Case 1: Disabled Widowers*

If you are disabled and between ages 50–59:

- You may be eligible for survivor benefits early.
- You will need to go through a disability review with SSA.
- You might need medical records and documentation from your doctor.

It's not automatic — but it is worth pursuing if you qualify.

### *Special Case 2: Self-Employed or Sporadic Work History*

If your spouse was self-employed (dentists, small business owners, consultants):

- Social Security credits were earned through self-employment taxes.
- If taxes were unpaid or underreported, the survivor benefit may be smaller.
- Some professions (like certain government jobs) have different Social Security participation rules.

Always ask SSA to review your spouse's full earnings record.
Mistakes happen — and corrections can be made even after death.

## Real-World Story: "Robert's Journey"

Robert lost his wife, Karen, after 39 years of marriage.

Karen had worked part-time as a school librarian and had a modest Social Security record.

Robert:

- Applied for survivor benefits at age 61.
- Chose to take the reduced amount because he needed steady monthly income now, rather than waiting.
- Later, he reviewed his own retirement options and switched to a higher personal benefit at age 70.

Robert says survivor benefits gave him "permission to take his time" with big financial decisions, rather than feeling trapped or desperate.

You deserve that permission too.

## Closing Reflection: Steady Hands, Strong Heart

Claiming Social Security survivor benefits is not just a financial act.

It's an emotional one too.

It's a declaration that:

- You are still here.
- Your life still matters.
- The work you and your spouse did together still provides security, dignity, and hope.

Take the time you need.

Ask every question you need.

Know that survivor benefits are not a handout — they are a right, earned through love, sacrifice, and years of life lived side by side.

# Survivor Benefits Quick Checklist

*(for Widowers)*

# Survivor Benefits Quick Checklist

Use this simple checklist after your spouse's passing to help organize your next steps for Social Security survivor benefits.

Move at your own pace.

You are not behind.

## Within the First 30 Days:

- Order multiple certified copies of your spouse's death certificate (at least 10).
- Locate your marriage certificate.
- Locate your spouse's Social Security number and your own.
- Locate your spouse's recent earnings history (W-2s, tax returns, or SSA statement).

## Apply for Survivor Benefits:

- Call Social Security at 1-800-772-1213 to schedule a survivor benefits interview.
- (You cannot apply online.)
- Gather necessary documents for the appointment:
- Death certificate
- Marriage certificate
- Social Security numbers
- Birth certificates (if caring for minor children)
- Tax returns (optional but helpful)

### During Your SSA Appointment:

- Confirm your eligibility for survivor benefits based on your spouse's work record.
- Ask what your monthly payment will be if you start now vs. later.
- Ask whether you can switch to your own retirement benefit later if it's higher.

### After the Appointment:

- Review the award letter you receive carefully for errors.
- Set up direct deposit for your survivor benefits.
- Create a reminder to revisit your financial plan once benefits begin.

## Questions to Ask at the SSA Appointment Guide

*(for Widowers)*

## Questions to Ask at Your Survivor Benefits Appointment

When you meet with Social Security, it can feel overwhelming.

Having questions prepared ahead of time helps you stay calm, focused, and in control.

Bring this list with you.

### About Eligibility:

- Based on my spouse's work history, am I eligible for monthly survivor benefits?
- If I am also eligible for my own retirement benefit, which one should I claim first?

## About Timing:

- What is my Full Retirement Age (FRA) for survivor benefits?
- How much would my survivor benefit be if I claim now?
- How much would it be if I wait until my Full Retirement Age?
- Can I switch later from survivor benefits to my own retirement benefit?

## About Payments:

- When will my first payment arrive?
- Will I receive any retroactive benefits?
- How will payments be made (direct deposit)?

## About Other Considerations:

- If I'm still working, will that affect my survivor benefits?
- What happens to my survivor benefit if I remarry?
- If I become disabled later, can I qualify for additional assistance?
- Will my survivor benefits affect my taxes?

## Before You Leave:

- Confirm that SSA has the correct mailing address and banking information.
- Ask how to create an online "my Social Security" account for easier future updates.

**Closing Reminder:**

You deserve clear answers.

If something is confusing, ask the representative to explain it again — in plain language.

## What to Bring to Your Social Security Appointment

When you go to your Social Security appointment — whether it's over the phone or in person — having the right documents ready will make the process smoother and less stressful.

Here's a simple list:

### Personal Identification

- Your own Social Security number and card (if available)
- Government-issued photo ID (driver's license, state ID, or passport)

### Information About Your Spouse

- Your spouse's full name (as it appears on their Social Security records)
- Your spouse's Social Security number
- Certified copy of your spouse's death certificate
- Copy of your marriage certificate (to prove your relationship)
- Your spouse's birth certificate (if available — not always required, but helpful)

### Financial and Work History

- Your spouse's most recent W-2 forms or tax returns
- A copy of your spouse's Social Security Statement (if you have it)
- A list of employers for the past 2 years (for both you and your spouse)

### Banking Information

- Bank account and routing numbers for direct deposit

## Additional (if applicable)

- Birth certificates for minor or disabled children in your care
- Proof of disability if you are applying as a disabled widow(er)
- Divorce decree (if you were divorced and married for at least 10 years)

## Reminder:

- It's okay if you don't have every document perfectly.
- Bring what you have.
- SSA can often help you track down missing pieces.

You are allowed to ask for clarification at any point.

This is your financial future — you deserve clear answers.

## Sample Script for Calling Social Security

*(for Widowers)*

## Sample Script: Calling Social Security to Request a Survivor Benefits Appointment

Sometimes the hardest part is making the first call.

Use this simple script to help guide the conversation calmly and confidently.

**When the agent answers:**

"Hello, my name is [Your Name].

I recently lost my spouse, [Spouse's Name], and I would like to schedule an appointment to apply for Social Security survivor benefits.

I would appreciate any help you can give me in setting up the next steps."

**If they ask for more details:**

"My spouse passed away on [Date of Death].

I have our marriage certificate, death certificate, and Social Security numbers ready.

I would prefer [a phone appointment / an in-person appointment] if possible."

**If they ask if you are ready to apply right away:**

"I would like to first speak with someone about my options before making any final decisions, especially regarding timing and benefit amounts."

**Before you end the call, confirm:**

- Date and time of your appointment
- Whether it will be in-person or over the phone
- What documents they recommend you bring
- How early you should arrive if it's an in-person meeting

## Closing Reminder:

You are not expected to know everything today.

You are simply taking the first courageous step to protect yourself financially.

And that's something to be proud of.

## Widower's Glossary of Social Security Terms

*(Plain Language for Emotional Clarity)*

## Widower's Glossary of Social Security Terms

Sometimes Social Security uses confusing words that make a hard season feel even heavier.

Here's a simple guide you can use — no legalese, no pressure, just clear meaning.

## Survivor Benefits

Monthly payments you may be entitled to after your spouse passes away, based on their work record under Social Security.

## Lump-Sum Death Benefit

A small one-time payment ($255) that may be paid to a surviving spouse or child after a worker's death.

You must apply for it separately.

## Full Retirement Age (FRA)

The age at which you are entitled to full, unreduced survivor benefits.

Depending on your birth year, this is between 66 and 67 years old.

## Reduced Survivor Benefits

If you start collecting survivor benefits before your Full Retirement Age (as early as 60), the monthly amount will be lower permanently.

## Delayed Retirement Credits

If you delay starting your **own** retirement benefits past your FRA, you can earn "delayed credits" — meaning your personal benefit amount goes up.

*Note: Survivor benefits do not increase with delayed credits — only retirement benefits do.*

## Disability Benefits (SSDI)

Monthly payments to individuals who cannot work due to a qualifying disability.

As a widower, you may qualify for **disabled widow(er)'s benefits** starting at age 50 if you meet disability criteria.

### Child-in-Care Benefits

Survivor benefits available to a widow(er) at any age who is caring for the deceased spouse's child under age 16 (or a disabled child).

### Proof of Death

Usually a certified death certificate, required to apply for survivor benefits or the lump-sum death payment.

### Application for Survivor Benefits

The official process of contacting Social Security, submitting your documents, and completing an interview to start receiving survivor benefits.

### Retroactive Payments

Payments you may be entitled to for months before you applied — usually limited to six months for survivor benefits.

**Closing Reminder:**

These are just words.

You are the one living the reality — and you are doing an incredible job navigating it.

Take one definition, one conversation, one day at a time.

## Timeline of Survivor Benefits (First 12 Months After Applying)

## What Happens After You Apply for Survivor Benefits: A Gentle Timeline

You may wonder:

*"What happens after I apply? When does the money start? What should I expect?"*

Here's a simple month-by-month guide so you can feel more confident moving forward.

### Month 1: Application Submitted

- You call SSA or meet with them to apply.
- You provide necessary documents (death certificate, marriage certificate, Social Security numbers).
- SSA starts verifying your spouse's work record and your eligibility.

### Month 2: Award Decision

- You receive a formal letter ("award notice") explaining whether you were approved.
- The letter tells you how much you'll receive each month.
- If eligible, your payments will be scheduled via direct deposit.

### Month 3: First Payment

- Survivor benefits typically begin the month after you applied (not backdated to date of death unless within special limits).
- Payments arrive monthly, on the date matching your spouse's birthdate.

### Month 4–6: Adjustment Period

- SSA may make minor corrections to the amount if needed.
- You should verify each deposit matches your award letter.
- You can set up an online "My Social Security" account to manage everything digitally.

### Month 6–9: Tax Considerations

- You receive a SSA-1099 form early in the year for tax reporting.
- Some survivor benefits may be taxable depending on your total income.
- Consult a CPA if you have questions (widowers often qualify for special tax treatment in the first two years after death).

### Month 9–12: Ongoing Monitoring

- Keep SSA updated if:
- You change addresses
- You remarry (special rules apply if remarriage happens before 60)
- Your caregiving situation changes (child turns 16, etc.)
- Review your own long-term financial plan: Should you continue with survivor benefits indefinitely, or eventually switch to your own retirement benefit?

## Closing Reminder:

- Survivor benefits are a bridge, not a burden.
- Take your time adjusting to the new rhythm.
- Ask questions whenever you need.
- You are not expected to walk this road alone.

## Sample "First Conversation" Script with a Financial Advisor

*(For Widowers Discussing Survivor Benefits)*

## First Conversation Script: Talking to Your Financial Advisor About Survivor Benefits

Having your first conversation with a financial advisor after loss can feel overwhelming.

You don't have to have all the answers.

You just need the courage to start the conversation.

Here's a simple script you can use:

**Opening the Conversation:**

"Hi, I'm just starting to put the pieces together after my spouse's passing.

I want to make sure I understand how my Social Security survivor benefits fit into my bigger financial picture.

Would you be able to help me walk through it at my own pace?"

**Topics to Bring Up:**

- "Can we go over what monthly income I'll be receiving from survivor benefits?"
- "Will claiming survivor benefits now affect my ability to claim my own Social Security later?"
- "How should I factor these benefits into my overall retirement plan?"
- "Are there tax implications I need to prepare for?"
- "If I also have life insurance proceeds or savings, how do survivor benefits interact with those?"
- "Should I be thinking about delaying other income sources to maximize benefits?"

**Before You Leave:**

- "What documents should I bring next time so we can map this out clearly?"
- "Can you help me build a simple financial plan for the next 6 to 12 months?"
- "If questions come up later, is it okay if I email or call?"

## Closing Reminder:

You are not expected to figure everything out in one meeting.

This is about building steady, clear support — not rushing into decisions.

## Common Mistakes to Avoid When Claiming Survivor Benefits

*(For Widowers — Gentle Guidance)*

## Common Mistakes Widowers Should Avoid When Claiming Survivor Benefits

Social Security survivor benefits can be a major source of support — but there are common mistakes that can cause delays, missed money, or unnecessary stress.

Here's what to watch out for:

### 1. Waiting Too Long to Apply

- Survivor benefits aren't automatic.
- If you delay contacting SSA, you could lose months of income.
- Retroactive payments are usually capped at six months.

**Action Tip:**

Aim to apply within 30–60 days after your spouse's passing.

## 2. Claiming Too Early Without Understanding the Reductions

- You can claim as early as 60, but your monthly payment will be permanently reduced if you claim before your Full Retirement Age (66–67).
- For some widowers, waiting a few years could mean hundreds of dollars more each month for life.

**Action Tip:**

Ask SSA to show you estimates for claiming now versus waiting.

## 3. Not Understanding the Switching Options

- Some widowers qualify for both survivor benefits and their own Social Security retirement benefits.
- You might be able to start with survivor benefits and later switch to a higher retirement benefit, or vice versa.

**Action Tip:**

Ask your SSA representative about **coordinating survivor and retirement benefits**.

## 4. Missing Documents

- Missing marriage certificates, birth certificates, or Social Security numbers can delay your application.
- SSA requires formal documentation to process claims.

**Action Tip:**

Prepare a document checklist before your appointment.

### 5. Ignoring Tax Implications

- Depending on your total income, a portion of your survivor benefits could be taxable.
- It's better to plan for this now than to be surprised at tax time.

**Action Tip:**

Talk to a CPA or tax advisor during your first year of claiming benefits.

### 6. Assuming Everything Will Be Handled Automatically

- Financial accounts, property titles, and other benefits won't adjust themselves automatically just because you're receiving survivor benefits.
- You'll still need to actively manage other parts of your financial life.

**Action Tip:**

Build a complete financial plan, not just a survivor benefits plan.

## Closing Encouragement:

Mistakes happen — but they are not the end of your story.

Every question you ask, every piece of paperwork you gather, every choice you make —

is another brick in the strong, steady future you are building.

You are not expected to be perfect.

You are only asked to be present, patient, and proud of the steps you're taking.

## Survivor Benefits Decision Timeline: Key Ages and Choices

You may wonder:

*"When should I claim survivor benefits? How does my age affect my options?"*

Here's a simple timeline to guide your thinking:

### Age 50

- If you are **disabled** and meet Social Security's definition of disability, you can apply for **disabled widow(er) survivor benefits**.

### Age 60

- Earliest age you can apply for **regular survivor benefits** as a widower.
- Your benefit amount will be **reduced permanently** (about 71.5% of the full amount if you claim now).
- Good option if you need steady income immediately.

### Age 62

- If you qualify for your **own Social Security retirement benefit**, you may also apply for that (separate from survivor benefits).
- Important: Taking your own benefit early **reduces** it permanently.

### Full Retirement Age (66–67 depending on your birth year)

- You can claim **full survivor benefits** with no reduction.
- If you started earlier, you will continue receiving the reduced amount.
- If you waited, you now unlock 100% of your spouse's eligible benefit.

## Age 70

- **Survivor benefits do not grow** after your Full Retirement Age.
- Only your **own retirement benefit** grows between FRA and 70.
- Strategy Tip: Some widowers claim survivor benefits early, then switch to their own maximized retirement benefit at 70 if it's higher.

## Special Situations to Remember:

- **Caring for children under 16 or disabled?**
- You can claim caregiver survivor benefits at any age.
- **Remarrying before 60?**
- You may lose eligibility for survivor benefits (with some exceptions).
- **Remarrying after 60?**
- You can usually keep your survivor benefits.

## Closing Reminder:

There is no one "right" path.

The right choice depends on **your financial needs**, **your health**, and **your long-term goals**.

Move thoughtfully.

Ask questions.

You are allowed to choose what serves your peace — not just your paycheck.

## Survivor Benefits: Myths vs Facts

*(Gentle Truths for Widowers)*

## Survivor Benefits: Myths vs Facts

When you're grieving and trying to rebuild, it's easy to hear a lot of half-truths, bad advice, and myths about Social Security.

Here's a gentle clearing of the air —
what's true, what's not, and what you really need to know.

### Myth #1: "Survivor benefits happen automatically."

**Fact:**

You must **apply** for survivor benefits.

They are not triggered automatically after your spouse's death.

### Myth #2: "If I remarry, I lose all survivor benefits forever."

**Fact:**

If you remarry **before age 60**, you generally cannot collect survivor benefits based on your deceased spouse's record.

If you remarry **after age 60**, you usually can still collect.

### Myth #3: "If I work while collecting survivor benefits, I'll lose them completely."

**Fact:**

If you are under Full Retirement Age and earn above certain limits, some benefits may be temporarily withheld — but **they are not lost forever**.

Once you reach Full Retirement Age, you will receive your full monthly benefit.

## Myth #4: "Survivor benefits grow if I wait until age 70."

**Fact:**

**Only your own retirement benefits** grow from age 66–70.

**Survivor benefits** max out at Full Retirement Age (66–67 depending on your birth year).

Waiting beyond that **does not** increase your survivor benefit.

## Myth #5: "My survivor benefits and my own retirement benefits can be collected at the same time."

**Fact:**

You cannot receive both full benefits at once.

Social Security will pay you the higher of the two — not stack them.

Sometimes you can **claim one type** first and **switch later** to maximize lifetime income.

## Closing Reminder:

You are allowed to double-check anything you hear — even from well-meaning friends or family.

You deserve clear, correct information to make strong choices for your future.

Ask questions.

Trust yourself.

Move at your own healing pace.

## Planning Ahead: Protecting Your Financial Future After Loss

*(For Widowers)*

## Planning Ahead: Building Strength After the Storm

You didn't ask to become an expert in finances.

You didn't want to rebuild your life from the ground up.

But here you are — standing in the middle of a new beginning.

And now you have an opportunity:

**To protect yourself.**

**To plan wisely.**

**To build stability — and even hope — into your future.**

Here's how.

### Step 1: Understand Your Full Income Picture

After claiming survivor benefits:

- Map out all monthly income sources (survivor benefits, retirement accounts, life insurance payouts, pensions, employment income).
- Build a basic monthly budget covering essentials (housing, food, transportation, insurance).

**Action Step:**

Create a simple "Income and Expenses Snapshot" for the next 6–12 months.

### Step 2: Protect Your Social Security Choices

- If you are eligible for both survivor and retirement benefits, explore strategies to maximize lifetime benefits (for example, starting survivor benefits now and switching to your own at age 70).
- Monitor annual Social Security letters for any changes or errors.
- Keep SSA updated about major life changes (new address, remarriage, children).

**Action Step:**

Set a reminder once a year to review your Social Security status.

## Step 3: Review and Update Legal Documents

After loss, it's critical to:

- Update your **will** and **trust documents**.
- Update **powers of attorney** for finances and healthcare.
- Review and update all **beneficiary designations** (on retirement accounts, life insurance, and bank accounts).

**Action Step:**

Meet with an estate planning attorney to refresh and protect your new wishes.

## Step 4: Rebuild Your Financial Safety Net

- Rebuild or create an emergency fund (3–6 months of essential expenses).
- Review your life, health, auto, and homeowners insurance.
- Consider whether long-term care insurance fits your future plans.

**Action Step:**

Set a goal to rebuild savings gradually, even small amounts monthly.

## Step 5: Give Yourself Permission to Dream Again

Grief doesn't mean your dreams stop forever.

As you rebuild:

- Think about travel goals, hobbies, downsizing, moving closer to family, giving back to causes you care about.

- Your new financial plan should reflect not just survival — but **purpose** and **joy**.

**Action Step:**

Write down one thing you would like to experience or build financially in the next 5 years — no matter how small.

## Closing Encouragement:

Planning ahead isn't cold.

It's not selfish.

It's a way of honoring the life you shared — and claiming the life you still have ahead.

Every dollar you manage wisely, every decision you make thoughtfully, is a powerful, hopeful step into your new story.

## Questions to Ask an Estate Attorney

*(For Widowers — Clear and Compassionate)*

## Questions to Ask an Estate Attorney After the Loss of a Spouse

Hiring an estate attorney isn't just for "the rich."

It's a wise, powerful step to protect what you and your spouse built — and to make sure your next chapter is legally and financially safe.

You don't have to know legal jargon.

You don't have to pretend you understand everything.

You just need to ask the right questions, one steady step at a time.

Here's a simple guide to help you:

### About Your Spouse's Estate:

- Is probate required for my spouse's assets?
- How long does probate typically take in my state?
- What assets will pass outside of probate?
- How do I access joint accounts or property titled only in my spouse's name?
- Do I need to open a special estate account to manage assets during probate?

### About Legal Documents:

- Is the will or trust my spouse left still legally valid?
- What are my immediate legal responsibilities as a surviving spouse?
- If there was no will, what happens next?
- How do I make sure my spouse's debts are handled correctly and fairly?

## About Your Own Estate Planning:

- Should I update my own will and powers of attorney now?
- How do I update beneficiary designations on retirement accounts and insurance policies?
- Should I create a living trust to protect my future heirs?

## About Taxes and Financial Impact:

- Am I responsible for any estate or inheritance taxes?
- How do I handle my spouse's final income tax return?
- Should I meet with a CPA to help coordinate taxes and estate issues?

## Before You Leave:

- What paperwork or documents should I gather before our next meeting?
- Are there deadlines I need to know about (for probate, taxes, asset transfers)?
- Can you recommend any other professionals I may need (CPA, financial advisor, etc.)?

# Closing Reminder:

You are not supposed to already know these answers.

You are not expected to walk this path alone.

Asking good questions is **an act of protection** — and an act of love, both for yourself and for your family.

You are doing better than you think.

## One-Year Financial Healing Timeline

*(For Widowers — Gentle Progress After Loss)*

## Your First Year of Financial Healing After Loss

Healing your financial life after loss isn't a race.

It's a steady walk through uncertainty toward new security and new purpose.

Here's a month-by-month guide —

**not as pressure, but as quiet encouragement** for your journey.

### Month 1–2: Stabilize

- Gather important documents (death certificates, marriage certificates, wills, account statements).
- Notify Social Security, banks, insurance companies.
- Freeze unnecessary auto-payments and secure accounts.
- Pay only essential monthly bills.
- Set up a small "Financial Folder" or binder — no fancy system needed yet.

### Month 3–4: Organize

- Apply for survivor benefits from Social Security.
- Apply for any life insurance payouts.
- Identify all assets (bank accounts, investment accounts, property).
- Identify all debts (mortgage, credit cards, loans).
- Create a basic cash flow snapshot: income vs essential expenses.

## Month 5–6: Protect

- Meet with an estate attorney to review the will, trust, and probate needs.
- Retitle property (home, vehicles, bank accounts) into your name as needed.
- Secure health insurance coverage.
- Begin creating or rebuilding an emergency fund (even small amounts matter).

## Month 7–8: Plan

- Consult with a financial advisor to create a basic 12-month survival and rebuilding plan.
- Review beneficiary designations on retirement accounts and insurance policies.
- Reassess insurance needs (life, health, auto, homeowners).

## Month 9–10: Strengthen

- Complete probate or trust administration steps if possible.
- Start a gentle review of longer-term retirement and investment plans.
- Rebuild financial confidence: one small decision, one small win at a time.

## Month 11–12: Reflect and Renew

- Reflect: What financial steps have you completed this year?
- Revisit goals for the next year (saving, giving, traveling, moving, etc.).
- Update your will and powers of attorney to reflect your new reality.
- Celebrate your survival — not just your financial survival, but your emotional one too.

## Closing Encouragement:

There is no straight line through grief.

There is no perfect financial healing timeline.

But every decision you make, every question you ask, every quiet act of courage you take —

is rebuilding something sacred: your life, your future, and your peace.

## Widower's First Year Financial Calendar

*(Simple Month-by-Month Checklist)*

## Your First Year Financial Calendar: A Gentle Guide

This isn't a rigid schedule.

It's a *companion* to help you move forward, step by step, through financial rebuilding after loss.

Each month, check off what you can.

Give yourself grace for what you can't.

Healing is progress, too.

### Month 1

- Order 10–20 certified copies of your spouse's death certificate.
- Notify Social Security Administration.
- Notify banks, insurance companies, and employers.
- Review and pay only essential bills.
- Create a "Financial Folder" for key documents.

## Month 2

- Apply for Social Security survivor benefits.
- Apply for life insurance claims (if applicable).
- List monthly income sources and current essential expenses.
- Pause non-essential subscriptions and auto-payments.

## Month 3

- Meet briefly with an estate attorney (even if you think it's "simple").
- Locate or begin the probate process if necessary.
- Confirm health insurance coverage going forward.
- Start building a very basic emergency fund (even $50 at a time).

## Month 4

- Make a list of assets and debts.
- Confirm beneficiaries on retirement accounts.
- Secure or retitle key assets (bank accounts, vehicles, real estate).
- Breathe: you are making real progress.

## Month 5

- Review life insurance, auto, and homeowners' insurance needs.
- Contact a CPA if needed to prepare for taxes.
- Track your monthly cash flow — even loosely.

## Month 6

- Reassess your basic monthly budget.
- Set 1–2 simple financial goals for the next 6 months.
- Reflect: What has surprised you about your strength?

## Month 7

- Review survivor benefit payments for accuracy.
- Consider consulting a financial advisor about long-term planning.
- Celebrate a financial win, no matter how small.

## Month 8

- Begin reviewing options for retirement savings, if appropriate.
- Think about charitable giving or legacy planning if it feels right.

## Month 9

- Finalize estate administration if probate is nearing completion.
- Update your own will and powers of attorney.
- Consider a new emergency fund goal (ex: 3–6 months of expenses).

## Month 10

- Reflect on your long-term living situation: stay, move, downsize?
- Adjust your budget if income or expenses have changed.

## Month 11

- Review all financial accounts once again for completeness.
- Begin gentle year-end tax planning (with CPA help if needed).

## Month 12

- Celebrate: You have survived a year of financial rebuilding.
- Write a letter to yourself about what you have learned.
- Set one new dream for your next chapter — financial or personal.

## Closing Reminder:

This year wasn't about perfection.

It was about survival, rebuilding, and rediscovering your own resilience.

You are stronger — and wiser — than you were a year ago.

## Letter to Myself One Year After Loss

*(A Deeply Healing Personal Exercise)*

## Letter to Myself: One Year After Losing My Spouse

*(Widowers are encouraged to write their own version — this is a template they can start from.)*

Dear [Your Name],

Today marks one year since my life changed forever.

One year since the world stopped making sense,

since everything familiar felt fragile,

since I had to figure out how to breathe again, one day at a time.

And yet — here I am.

Here I am, standing where I once thought I would fall.

Here I am, paying bills, handling paperwork, rebuilding a life I never asked to rebuild.

Here I am, carrying both the grief and the courage it takes to move forward.

In the past year:

- I made decisions I never wanted to make — and I made them anyway.
- I asked for help when I needed it — and that was strength, not weakness.
- I protected the life we built together — and I honored the life that still remains.

I faced long nights and longer paperwork.

I endured anniversaries, birthdays, holidays that felt empty.

I made mistakes, and I forgave myself for them.

I am not the same man I was one year ago.

I am stronger.

I am wiser.

I am more tender, and more tough, than I ever thought I could be.

There is still healing to be done.

There are still hard days ahead.

But there are also still reasons to hope, to build, and to love — even in the quiet, even in the ache.

I am allowed to dream again.

I am allowed to rebuild not just a financial future — but a meaningful one.

I am allowed to live fully, carrying everything we shared, and everything I am still becoming.

Today, I honor the love we had —

and I honor the man I am becoming because of it.

I am proud of myself.

And I am grateful to still be here.

One breath, one step, one year at a time.

With strength and hope,

[Your Name]

## Financial Reflection: One Year After Loss

You made it through the first year.

That's not just survival — that's *strength.*

Take a quiet moment to reflect on where you've been, where you are, and where you want to go.

There are no right or wrong answers — only your truth.

### 1. What financial steps am I proud of this past year?

(Even small ones — like calling Social Security, updating one account, or building an emergency fund.)

### 2. What financial tasks still feel unfinished or unclear?

(Write them down — naming them reduces their weight.)

### 3. How has my monthly cash flow changed over the past year?

- Income: ________________________________________
- Expenses: ________________________________________

(You don't need a spreadsheet — just a simple snapshot.)

### 4. What was the hardest financial decision I had to make?

What did I learn about myself from it?

### 5. What unexpected financial blessing or opportunity showed up?

(A refund, a gift, a job offer, a realization?)

### 6. Who are the trusted professionals or people who helped me financially this year?

(Advisor, attorney, friend, family, CPA — anyone.)

7. What is one financial habit I want to build in the next year?

(Saving, budgeting, investing, giving?)

8. What is one financial worry I'm ready to let go of?

(You're allowed to move lighter into the next chapter.)

9. What does "financial peace" mean to me now, compared to a year ago?

10. If I could give my newly-widowed self one message from today, what would it be?

## Closing Reflection:

You are not where you started.
You are stronger, wiser, and more capable than you were one year ago.
And your best chapters — financial and personal — are still ahead.

## Widower's Financial Milestones Roadmap

*(1-Year, 3-Year, 5-Year Healing and Growth Goals)*

## Widower's Financial Milestones Roadmap

Healing financially after loss isn't just about paying bills.
It's about building a future where you feel secure, hopeful, and free.
Here's a simple roadmap to guide your growth —
with compassion for where you are today, and optimism for where you're going.

## Year 1: Stabilize and Secure

- Claim Social Security survivor benefits.
- Settle your spouse's estate (probate, trusts, titles).
- Secure and retitle key assets (bank accounts, real estate).
- Build or rebuild an emergency fund (even $500–$1,000 at first).
- Create a simple, sustainable monthly budget.
- Meet with a trusted estate attorney and/or financial advisor.
- Update your own will, healthcare directives, and beneficiaries.
- Begin dreaming about what you might want for your next chapter — no pressure.

## Year 3: Strengthen and Grow

- Grow your emergency fund to cover 3–6 months of essential expenses.
- Review retirement savings strategies (401(k), IRA, Roth options).
- Consider simple, low-risk investing if appropriate for your goals.
- Review insurance needs (health, home, auto, long-term care).
- Reassess living situation: stay, downsize, relocate closer to loved ones.
- Explore giving back if you feel ready (volunteering, small charitable gifts).
- Set one major personal goal (travel, education, starting a small business, etc.).

## Year 5: Expand and Enrich

- Strengthen or complete full retirement planning.
- Complete legacy planning (trusts, charitable giving, personal letters or wishes).
- Move from "financial survival" to "financial freedom" — meaning:
- Your money works for you
- Your life reflects your values and dreams
- You feel empowered, not trapped, by your financial choices

- Celebrate milestones — emotionally, financially, and spiritually.

## Closing Encouragement:

There is no set clock on healing.

There is only *your* pace, *your* strength, and *your* future.

Each small step you take today creates a stronger, wiser, freer version of yourself tomorrow.

You are building not just a new financial life —

you are building a new story, full of dignity, resilience, and hope.

## Financial Freedom Checklist for Widowers

You may not realize it yet, but every small financial step you've taken —

every document you organized, every bill you paid, every plan you updated —

has been slowly moving you from **survival mode** to **freedom mode.**

Here's how to tell you're making that powerful transition:

### Stability

- I know where my income is coming from each month.
- I have a basic monthly budget — and I can stick to it with flexibility.
- I have an emergency fund (even a small one).

### Control

- I have retitled major assets (bank accounts, vehicles, real estate) in my name.
- I know who my beneficiaries are — and they're updated.
- I have a current will, healthcare directive, and powers of attorney.

### Confidence

- I made financial decisions this year without paralyzing fear.
- I know who to call (advisor, attorney, CPA) if I have questions.
- I feel more confident managing my finances than I did one year ago.

### Growth

- I am rebuilding or growing retirement savings.
- I understand my survivor benefits and how they fit into my future plans.
- I am planning for future dreams (travel, giving, moving, hobbies).

### Generosity

- I have thought about ways to give back, honor my spouse's memory, or support causes I care about.
- I am considering (or already have) a plan to leave a financial or emotional legacy.

## Closing Reminder:

Financial freedom after loss isn't about wealth.

It's about *peace.*

It's about waking up in the morning knowing you are secure — and your life still matters deeply.

You are doing better than you think.

Keep going.

## Financial Legacy Letter Template

*(Widowers Passing on Wisdom, Not Just Wealth)*

## My Financial Legacy Letter

*(You can use this template to write a letter to your children, grandchildren, nieces, nephews, or anyone you love.)*

Dear [Name(s)],

Today I want to share something more valuable than money.

I want to share lessons — lessons built from love, loss, rebuilding, and hope.

Money is important.

But *how you live, how you give,* and *how you honor your life* is even more important.

Here are a few things I want you to know:

### About Money:

- Spend less than you earn. Always. Even when it's hard.
- Save early. Even small amounts grow into something powerful with time.
- Protect what you build — through insurance, careful planning, and wise choices.
- Avoid debts that steal your peace of mind.
- Give generously when you can. Money given with love multiplies beyond dollars.

### About Life:

- You are not measured by the balance in your bank account — you are measured by the balance in your heart.
- There will be seasons when life breaks you open — financially, emo-

tionally, spiritually.
- It's okay to ask for help. It's okay to start over. It's okay to rebuild, even when it feels impossible.

## About Legacy:

- Your real legacy is not what you leave *to* others — it's what you leave *in* them.
- I hope I have left you wisdom, courage, and permission to live fully.
- I hope you remember that money is a tool — not a master.

I am proud of you — for who you are now and who you are still becoming.

I hope you use the resources you have — time, talent, treasure — to build a life that makes you proud, too.

And if you ever feel lost financially, emotionally, or spiritually, remember this:

You come from a long line of survivors, dreamers, and builders.

You have everything it takes.

I love you.

Always,

[Your Name]

## Financial Self-Care Checklist for Widowers

Financial healing isn't just about numbers.

It's about giving yourself space — emotionally, mentally, spiritually — to move from survival toward peace.

Use this checklist to balance practical steps with emotional care:

## Managing Money

- I have a simple budget (even if it's imperfect).
- I check my accounts regularly without fear.
- I update important documents (wills, beneficiaries, powers of attorney).
- I build savings — even in small amounts — toward my future goals.
- I ask for help from trusted professionals when needed (advisor, CPA, attorney).

## Managing Emotions

- I forgive myself for financial mistakes — past or recent.
- I allow myself to grieve without judgment — grief can be messy and financial at the same time.
- I take breaks from financial tasks when needed without guilt.
- I recognize when emotions are driving financial decisions — and I pause before acting.
- I celebrate small financial wins, because they represent strength and rebuilding.

## Managing Energy

- I tackle financial tasks in small, manageable pieces — not all at once.
- I set boundaries with people who pressure me about money decisions.
- I rest without apology when finances feel overwhelming.
- I reward myself for completing difficult financial steps (even with simple comforts — a walk, a coffee, a nap).

# Closing Reminder:

Financial self-care is not about being perfect.

It's about being *kind* to yourself while you rebuild.

Your money is important.

Your healing is sacred.

## Both deserve your patience, your compassion, and your care.

## 10 Financial Promises I Make to Myself

You didn't choose this road.
But you can choose how you walk it now.
Here are 10 promises you can quietly, powerfully make to yourself — to rebuild your financial life with dignity, hope, and strength.

### 1. I promise to be patient with myself.

Financial healing is not a race.
I am allowed to move at my own pace.

### 2. I promise to face my finances honestly.

No more hiding, no more avoiding.
I face the numbers so I can change the story.

### 3. I promise to honor the work we did together.

Every dollar we saved, every sacrifice we made —
I protect it with care and respect.

### 4. I promise to ask for help when I need it.

Strong men and women ask questions.
They seek counsel.
They don't suffer in silence.

## 5. I promise to protect my peace over my possessions.

No decision is worth losing my peace of mind over.
I will choose simplicity, security, and clarity whenever possible.

## 6. I promise to plan for tomorrow, even when today is hard.

Hope is an act of rebellion against despair.
I will plan, even in small ways, for a future worth living.

## 7. I promise to rebuild, not just react.

I am not just putting out fires.
I am building something strong, steady, and meaningful.

## 8. I promise to forgive myself for what I didn't know.

Money is complicated.
Life is complicated.
I choose grace over shame, learning over regret.

## 9. I promise to dream again financially.

I am allowed to want good things: security, travel, giving, new memories.
Grief does not cancel my right to dream.

## 10. I promise to honor both my past and my future.

I carry my spouse's memory with me.
I also carry my own resilience.
I will live wisely, love deeply, and leave a legacy of both.

## Closing Reflection:

These promises aren't about perfection.

They're about permission —

to move, to heal, to grow,

to become the man or woman your spouse would be proud to see rebuilding.

You are not starting over empty.

You are starting over full — of love, of lessons, of a life still worth living.

## Widower's Financial Permission Slips

*(Gentle Emotional Reminders)*

## Financial Permission Slips for Widowers

Grief brings pressure — from society, family, even from inside your own head.

This page is your reminder:

**You are allowed to move through financial healing at your own pace, on your own terms.**

Here are your permission slips —

take as many as you need.

### Financial Permission Slip #1

**I am allowed to say, "I don't know yet."**

I don't have to rush decisions before I'm ready.

## Financial Permission Slip #2

**I am allowed to pause and rest.**

Handling money while grieving is exhausting.
Breaks are allowed — and necessary.

## Financial Permission Slip #3

**I am allowed to ask every question I need.**

There are no silly questions when protecting my future.

## Financial Permission Slip #4

**I am allowed to prioritize peace over perfection.**

A peaceful, sustainable plan is better than a rushed, complicated one.

## Financial Permission Slip #5

**I am allowed to change my mind.**

Healing and financial planning are not straight lines.
Adjustments are part of wisdom.

## Financial Permission Slip #6

**I am allowed to say "No."**

No to pressure.
No to rushed decisions.
No to people who don't have my best interests at heart.

### Financial Permission Slip #7

**I am allowed to celebrate small wins.**

Every bill paid, every form filled out, every tough phone call made — they all matter.

### Financial Permission Slip #8

**I am allowed to dream again financially.**

My future deserves hope — not just survival.

### Financial Permission Slip #9

**I am allowed to honor both my grief and my growth.**

They can exist side by side.
One does not cancel the other.

### Financial Permission Slip #10

**I am allowed to move forward at my own pace — not anyone else's.**

I am building a future worth living for, on my terms.

## Closing Encouragement:

You are already doing the hard work —
you are surviving, learning, healing, and growing.
Give yourself the permissions you need.
You are worthy of peace, patience, and prosperity.

## My Financial Wins Wall

You've walked through hard things this year.
You deserve to see, in black and white, just how far you've come.
Use this page to record every financial victory —
no matter how small, no matter how simple.
Each win is a brick in the foundation of your new life.

### Financial Wins I'm Proud Of:

-
-
-
-
-
-
-
-
-
-

## Prompts to Inspire You:

- I called Social Security and made my appointment.
- I gathered all important documents.
- I opened a new bank account in my own name.
- I updated my beneficiaries.
- I built an emergency fund (even $500).
- I asked for help when I needed it.
- I read one financial book or article that helped me.
- I celebrated paying a bill on time.
- I created a simple monthly budget.
- I forgave myself for one financial mistake.

## Closing Reflection:

There is no such thing as "small" progress.

Every step you take is a step toward security, stability, and strength.

Look at your wall.

Look at your wins.

They are proof:

You are surviving, rebuilding, and thriving.

## Next 90 Days: Your Financial Action Plan

You've made it through the hardest season.

Now it's time to move forward — not with pressure, but with *purpose.*

Here's a gentle action plan to help guide your next three months of financial rebuilding.

### Month 1: Review and Refresh

- Review your current monthly budget: Does it still fit your real life?
- Update income and expense estimates based on new needs or goals.
- Review your survivor benefits status: Are you maximizing what you're entitled to?
- Revisit your emergency fund goals: Can you increase savings even slightly?

### Month 2: Strengthen and Secure

- Check all financial accounts for correct ownership and beneficiary designations.
- Review your insurance coverage (health, home, auto, life): Are you still properly protected?
- Update your personal will, living will, and powers of attorney if you

haven't yet.

- Consult with a financial advisor if you have questions about investing, retirement planning, or longer-term goals.

## Month 3: Dream and Design

- Write down one new personal financial goal (short-term or long-term).
- Consider new dreams: Travel, downsizing, education, new hobbies, charity.
- Begin exploring ways to automate good financial habits (auto-saving, bill pay).
- Reward yourself for surviving and rebuilding — celebrate progress, not perfection.

## Closing Encouragement:

You are allowed to move slowly.
You are allowed to move boldly.
You are allowed to move however feels right to you.
The only thing you must not do —
is doubt that you are worthy of a strong, peaceful future.
You are building it, one wise step at a time.

## Widower's Personal Financial Motto Page

*(Write and Live by Your Own Philosophy)*

## My Personal Financial Motto

After loss, after chaos, after rebuilding —
you deserve a personal compass.
A clear, steady reminder of the man you are now — and the future you are creating.

Use this page to write your **Financial Motto** —
your personal guide for every financial choice from here forward.

## Questions to Help You Craft Your Motto:

- What financial values matter most to me now? (Ex: stability, freedom, generosity, responsibility)
- What mistakes or lessons do I want to honor without repeating?
- What do I want my financial decisions to reflect about the man I am becoming?
- What legacy do I want to leave, whether big or small?

## Sample Mottos:

- "I build my financial life with patience, wisdom, and hope."
- "I honor the past and secure the future by making steady, thoughtful decisions."
- "I am not rushed by fear or guilt. I choose financial peace every time."
- "I manage money to serve my life — not to control it."
- "I protect what matters. I plan with love. I live with courage."

## My Financial Motto:

## Closing Reflection:

Your motto isn't just for today.

It's for tomorrow.

For the hard moments, the uncertain moments, the powerful moments ahead.

It is your reminder:

You are no longer just surviving.

You are leading your life forward with strength, dignity, and heart.

# Chapter 4: Insurance Payouts, Policies, and Pitfalls

## Introduction: When a Check Arrives in the Middle of Heartbreak

It's one of the most surreal feelings after losing a spouse:

A check arrives. Or an insurance company calls.

Money is deposited into your account.

Life insurance.

Maybe it was expected. Maybe it was a surprise.

Either way, the swirl of emotions is real —

Gratitude. Guilt. Confusion. Fear. Responsibility.

You wonder:

- What do I do with this?
- What if I make a mistake?
- How do I honor their memory while protecting my future?

You are not alone.

This chapter is here to walk you through it, gently and clearly.

Not with pressure.

Not with complexity.

But with real steps and real care — so you can protect yourself while honoring your spouse's love.

Let's start where you are.

## Part 1: Understanding Life Insurance Payouts

When someone you love dies, life insurance is supposed to provide financial stability.

It's one way they tried to take care of you — even from beyond.

But understanding **what kind of payout** you've received — and what choices you now face — matters deeply.

### *The Types of Life Insurance You Might Encounter*

#### 1. Term Life Insurance

- Simple, straightforward insurance.
- Coverage for a set period (ex: 10, 20, or 30 years).
- If your spouse passed during the term, you receive a payout (death benefit).
- No complicated investment features. Just protection.

#### 2. Whole Life Insurance

- Permanent insurance — intended to last a lifetime.
- Combines life insurance coverage with a cash value account that grows over time.
- Payout at death is usually the stated death benefit, sometimes with a small added cash value.

#### 3. Universal Life Insurance

- Another form of permanent insurance.
- Flexible premiums and death benefits.

- May also build cash value over time.

**4. Annuities with Death Benefits**

- Sometimes a spouse had a deferred annuity or pension arrangement with a death benefit attached.
- You may receive either a lump sum or ongoing payments.
- Different rules apply compared to traditional life insurance.

### *How Payouts Typically Work*

When you're the named beneficiary:

- You file a **claim** with the insurance company.
- You provide a **death certificate** and any required claim forms.
- The insurer processes your claim (anywhere from a few days to several weeks).
- They issue your **payout** based on the policy's terms.

### *How Much Time Do You Have to File?*

- Most policies allow plenty of time — **one to two years** is typical.
- However, it's best to begin the process once you feel emotionally ready.

There is no prize for rushing.

There is no penalty for taking a deep breath first.

**Action Step:**

Locate all known life insurance policies (paperwork, emails, statements) and contact the companies to notify them of the death.

## Part 2: What to Do If You're Named a Beneficiary

Becoming a beneficiary is a privilege and a responsibility. Here's what you need to know — and do — next.

### *Step 1: Verify the Policy Details*

- Confirm you are listed as the **primary beneficiary**.
- Ask for a clear explanation of the death benefit amount.
- Ask if there are any policy loans, unpaid premiums, or adjustments that could affect the payout.

### *Step 2: Understand Your Payout Options*

Insurance companies usually offer you choices:

- **Lump Sum Payment:**
- You receive the entire death benefit at once.
- You can deposit it into your own bank account and manage it as you choose.
- **Annuity Payment:**
- The insurer keeps the money and pays you monthly or annually for a set number of years or for life.
- Sometimes includes guaranteed minimum payout periods.

### *Lump Sum vs. Annuity: Pros and Cons*

Lump Sum — Pros:

- Full control over your money immediately.
- Flexibility to invest, save, or use the funds as needed.
- No dependency on the insurance company's financial health.

Lump Sum — Cons:

- Temptation to spend unwisely if overwhelmed or grieving.
- You are responsible for managing investments, taxes, and risks.

Annuity — Pros:

- Provides predictable, steady income.
- Reduces the temptation to overspend in the early grief years.
- May offer guaranteed payments for life (depending on terms).

Annuity — Cons:

- Lower long-term returns compared to investing on your own.
- Less flexibility — you cannot withdraw a large sum in emergencies.
- Risk if the insurer becomes unstable (though rare).

**Action Step:**

Ask the insurer to **explain both options fully** — and request written projections before deciding.

Do not feel pressured to choose quickly.

You are allowed to pause, think, and get advice.

## Part 3: Special Considerations When Receiving Insurance Money

Receiving a large payout is emotionally complicated.

Here are important tips to protect yourself during this fragile time:

### *1. Do Not Rush Big Financial Decisions*

- Resist the urge to buy a new house, invest heavily, or give large gifts immediately.
- Let the money **sit** safely in a savings or money market account until you have a clear, calm plan.

### *2. Understand Taxes (Good News!)*

- **Life insurance death benefits are generally not taxable** as income.
- If the policy had cash value that generated investment income separately, that income may be taxable — but the death benefit itself usually isn't.

### *3. Reassess Your Insurance Needs*

- If your spouse carried insurance for your joint needs (like a mortgage), you may now need less coverage.
- If you still have dependents or obligations, review your own insurance coverage needs.

**Action Step:**

After receiving your payout, schedule a financial "pause session" — no big moves for 90 days.

Just planning, breathing, and protecting.

## Part 4: Scams to Avoid During This Time

Sadly, grief makes you vulnerable.

Scammers know this.

Here's what to watch out for:

### *Common Scams Targeting Widowers:*

- **Fake "investment advisors"** who pressure you to invest the payout quickly in shady products.
- **"Inheritance tax" scams** where someone falsely claims you owe taxes on the insurance payout (you don't).
- **Bogus "fees" for filing claims** — filing with a legitimate insurer should never cost you anything.
- **Aggressive salespeople** trying to sell expensive annuities, questionable real estate, or other "opportunities" right after loss.

### *How to Protect Yourself:*

- Hang up on unsolicited calls.
- Verify every professional's credentials independently.
- Never share personal information (SSN, bank account numbers) unless you initiated contact.
- Trust your instincts — if something feels off, it probably is.

**Action Step:**

Create a personal "cooling-off rule" — no financial decisions involving large sums of money for at least 30 days after first hearing about them.

## Part 5: Real-World Example — Tom's Story

Tom lost his wife suddenly at 63.

She had a $250,000 term life insurance policy.

Tom:

- Took a lump sum payout.
- Deposited it into a money market account while he processed his grief.
- Created a 2-year financial plan before touching the principal.
- Used part of it to pay off his mortgage, freeing up monthly cash flow.

- Invested conservatively once he felt emotionally ready.

Today, Tom says that **waiting** and **not rushing** his financial decisions were the two best choices he made.

You deserve that same breathing room and strength.

## Closing Reflection: Money Doesn't Replace Love — But It Can Protect Your Future

Your spouse didn't leave you life insurance because they thought money could ease your grief.

They left it because they loved you.

Because they wanted you to have safety, dignity, and freedom to heal.

Honor that love — not by rushing, not by fearing —

but by moving thoughtfully, carefully, and compassionately with this financial gift.

You are capable.

You are wise.

You are still building a future — one that holds both the memory of your shared life and the hope of your unfolding one.

You are not alone.

And you are not lost.

You are learning to lead yourself forward —

one step, one choice, one sacred new day at a time.

# Insurance Payout Action Checklist

*(What to Do When You Receive Life Insurance Money)*

## Insurance Payout Action Checklist

Receiving a life insurance payout after losing your spouse can feel overwhelming.

You don't have to rush.

You don't have to spend.

You don't have to decide everything today.

You just need a clear, calm path forward.

Here's a simple checklist to guide you:

### Step 1: Confirm the Payout Details

- Verify you are the named primary beneficiary.
- Confirm the total death benefit amount.
- Understand any outstanding loans, fees, or deductions that could impact the payout.

### Step 2: Choose Your Payout Option Thoughtfully

- Request a written explanation of all available payout options (lump sum vs annuity).
- Ask for projections or illustrations showing what monthly annuity payments would look like.
- Take time — you are allowed to think it through.

### Step 3: Receive the Money Safely

- If choosing a lump sum, direct deposit into a safe, insured account (checking, savings, money market).
- Do **not** invest or move the money into complicated accounts right away.
- Secure the funds with two-factor authentication on bank accounts.

### Step 4: Build a 90-Day Holding Plan

- Create a "Do Not Touch" rule: No major spending, gifting, or investing for 90 days.
- Set aside a portion (even a small one) in a separate savings account labeled **"Emergency Fund"**.

### Step 5: Protect the Payout

- Be wary of anyone offering "special investments" or "exclusive deals" because you've received a payout.
- Never make financial decisions based on fear or pressure.
- Trust, but verify — and take your time.

## Closing Reminder:

Life insurance money isn't just cash.
It's a final act of love —
designed to give you *space* and *security* to heal and rebuild your life.
Honor that love by moving carefully, thoughtfully, and proudly.

## Financial Scams to Watch Out for After Loss Guide

*(Widower's Edition)*

## Financial Scams to Watch Out for After Loss

Grief makes you vulnerable.
Sadly, some people see that vulnerability as an opportunity.
Here's a gentle, powerful guide to help you protect yourself.

1. "Too Good to Be True" Investment Scams

- **Red flag:** Someone contacts you out of the blue with a "can't lose" investment opportunity.
- **Protect yourself:** Legitimate advisors don't cold-call grieving families with miracle investments.

2. Fake IRS or Government Calls

- **Red flag:** Someone claims you owe taxes on your life insurance or inheritance.
- **Protect yourself:** The IRS never calls demanding immediate payment. Life insurance proceeds are usually tax-free.

3. "Inheritance Fees" or "Release Fees"

- **Red flag:** Someone asks for payment to "unlock" or "release" your life insurance money.
- **Protect yourself:** Legitimate life insurance claims never require you to pay upfront fees.

4. High-Pressure Annuity Sales

- **Red flag:** An insurance agent pressures you to roll over your payout into an expensive, long-term annuity immediately.
- **Protect yourself:** Take your time. Annuities can be good tools — but not under pressure and not without full understanding.

5. Bogus Charity Solicitations

- **Red flag:** A "charity" claims your spouse supported them and pressures you to donate now.
- **Protect yourself:** Research charities independently. Never feel guilt-

tripped into giving.

### 6. Identity Theft Attempts

- **Red flag:** You get strange bills, accounts opened in your name, or requests for personal information you didn't initiate.
- **Protect yourself:** Freeze your credit reports if necessary. Monitor your accounts closely.

## How to Protect Yourself Every Day:

- Hang up on unsolicited calls.
- Verify every offer or request independently — preferably after a 24-hour pause.
- Never rush because someone says "this is urgent" — real opportunities withstand scrutiny.
- Trust your instincts. If it feels wrong, it usually is.

## Closing Reflection:

Your financial safety is sacred.
It's part of rebuilding your life after loss.
You deserve **peace**, **dignity**, and **time** —
not fear, not manipulation.
You are stronger and wiser than any scammer expects.
You are building a future of stability, not chaos.
And you are never, ever alone.

# Part 2: Organizing and Understanding Your Finances

Losing a spouse leaves not only an emotional void but often a financial fog — one where bills pile up, accounts are scattered, and fear of making a mistake can feel paralyzing.

Part 2 of this book is your safe guide through that fog.

This section isn't about perfection.

It's about **stabilization** — gathering your financial pieces, understanding where you really stand, and creating the foundation for wise, steady decision-making.

You'll start by getting your arms around the basics:

What you own, what you owe, what's coming in, and what's going out.

No judgment. No pressure. Just simple, manageable steps to organize your financial life with clarity and confidence.

We'll walk you through essential topics like:

- Reviewing and understanding life insurance payouts and options.
- Navigating Social Security survivor benefits and when to claim.
- Identifying and protecting your own income sources.
- Gathering critical financial documents — and knowing what matters most.
- Evaluating debts, mortgages, and obligations so nothing sneaks up on you.
- Understanding retirement accounts, pensions, and investments left

behind.
- Spotting and avoiding financial scams that prey on grieving families.

Throughout Part 2, you'll also be gently encouraged to move at **your** pace —

whether that means tackling one item a week or sitting down for a focused afternoon.

This section is not about rushing into financial moves before you're ready.

It's about **building clarity, stability, and control** —

giving you the financial breathing room you need to grieve, heal, and envision a new future.

You'll also learn how to balance the technical side of money with the emotional side of loss.

Because understanding your finances isn't just about dollars —

it's about reclaiming your sense of agency, dignity, and hope.

By the end of Part 2, you won't have all the answers yet — and that's okay.

But you *will* have something even more powerful:

**A clear view of where you stand, a growing confidence in your ability to handle it, and a quiet pride in every step you've taken toward rebuilding.**

You are not broken.

You are rebuilding.

And this is where your financial foundation begins.

# Chapter 5: Taking Inventory – Your New Financial Picture

## Introduction: You Can't Heal What You Can't See

When life shatters, the natural instinct is to focus only on the urgent:
bills due today, phone calls piling up, the next appointment to survive.

But slowly, steadily, rebuilding requires something deeper.

It requires seeing — honestly, fully — where you actually stand.

Taking inventory of your financial life after loss isn't just about numbers.

It's about **ownership.**

It's about reclaiming clarity, stability, and control in a world that feels like it slipped out of your hands.

And you are ready.

Not because you feel ready — no one ever really does —

but because you have already survived what you thought you couldn't.

This chapter is about helping you *see* your new financial picture — piece by piece, gently, steadily — so you can rebuild a future that's not just survivable, but livable.

Let's begin.

## Why Taking Inventory Matters

You can't build a new foundation if you don't know what materials you have.

You need to know:

- What you **own** (your assets)
- What you **owe** (your liabilities)
- What's **coming in** (your income)
- What's **going out** (your expenses)

This isn't about judgment.

It's about knowledge.

And knowledge is power — quiet, steady, survivor's power.

## Step 1: Understanding Your Assets – What You Own Now

Assets are anything you own that has financial value.

When you lost your spouse, some assets might have changed:

- Property may have shifted ownership.
- Investment accounts may now be solely yours.
- Insurance payouts may have arrived.

Taking stock of your assets helps you understand what resources you have available — both for today and for your future.

### *Common Types of Assets to List:*

- **Bank accounts:** Checking, savings, money market accounts.
- **Retirement accounts:** 401(k)s, IRAs, Roth IRAs, pensions.
- **Investment accounts:** Brokerage accounts, mutual funds, stocks, bonds.

- **Real estate:** Primary home, rental properties, vacation homes.
- **Life insurance proceeds:** Lump sum or annuity payouts.
- **Personal property:** Vehicles, jewelry, collectibles, valuable belongings.
- **Other:** Business interests, royalties, inheritance, intellectual property.

### *Special Considerations for Widowers:*

- **Joint accounts:**
- If you shared joint accounts, check if they automatically transferred to your name.
- **Trust assets:**
- If your spouse had a trust, you may need legal help to transfer ownership properly.
- **Life insurance:**
- Ensure you understand if it's fully paid out or ongoing.

### *Real-World Example: John's Assets*

John lost his wife unexpectedly at 58.
When he sat down to list his assets, he found:

- $43,000 in joint checking and savings
- $330,000 in a 401(k) he inherited from her
- $250,000 life insurance payout
- A paid-off home valued at $280,000
- Two vehicles worth about $15,000 each

He hadn't realized before how much was actually secure —
because grief blurred everything.
Writing it down gave him the first real breath of calm he'd felt in months.
**Action Step:**
Create a simple written list of every asset you now own, even if it's messy at first.

## Step 2: Understanding Your Liabilities – What You Owe

Liabilities are your debts — money you owe to someone else. Knowing your liabilities clearly helps you:

- Prioritize what needs attention
- Avoid being blindsided later
- Build a debt-reduction plan that fits your new life

### *Common Types of Liabilities:*

- **Mortgage loans:** Home loans or second mortgages.
- **Auto loans:** Balances on financed vehicles.
- **Credit card debt:** Owed balances, even small ones.
- **Personal loans:** From banks, credit unions, or family.
- **Medical debt:** Especially if related to your spouse's final illness.
- **Other:** Student loans, business loans, tax debts.

### *Special Considerations for Widowers:*

- **Joint debt:**
- If you cosigned loans, you're still fully responsible even after your spouse's death.
- **Medical bills:**
- Laws vary by state about spousal responsibility for medical debts — consult an attorney if large balances exist.
- **Credit cards:**
- Authorized user accounts (where your name was added but you didn't own the card) typically don't impact you.
- Joint accounts do.

### *Real-World Example: Dave's Debts*

Dave discovered that after his wife's death, he was responsible for:

- $110,000 remaining on their mortgage
- $4,200 on a jointly-owned credit card
- $7,800 on a car loan she had cosigned with him

He was overwhelmed at first —

but listing it all gave him a **starting line** instead of endless anxiety.

**Action Step:**

Create a written list of every liability you're responsible for, including balances, due dates, and minimum payments.

## Step 3: Understanding Your Income – What's Coming In Now

Your income sources may have changed dramatically.

Where once there were two incomes, now there may be one — or partial benefits.

Understanding your new income gives you the ability to:

- Build a sustainable new budget
- Plan how to meet needs (and wants) without panic
- Make wise timing decisions around Social Security, pensions, or investments

### *Common Sources of Income After Loss:*

- **Social Security survivor benefits**
- **Personal retirement income:** 401(k) or IRA withdrawals
- **Pension income (yours or survivor benefits from spouse's pension)**
- **Employment income (if you are still working)**

- **Life insurance proceeds (if structured as annuity payments)**
- **Rental income (if you own rental property)**
- **Business income (if you own part of a business)**

*Special Considerations for Widowers:*

- **Survivor benefits:**
- Social Security rules allow widowers to claim survivor benefits as early as age 60 (earlier if disabled or caring for a child).
- **Pension options:**
- Some pensions offer continued payments to surviving spouses — but you need to contact the plan administrator to activate it.
- **Required Minimum Distributions (RMDs):**
- If you inherited a retirement account and are over 73, required distributions may apply.

**Action Step:**

List all sources of regular income you now have, even if small.

Include when each income source starts and ends (if applicable).

## Step 4: Understanding Your Expenses – What's Changed, and What Will Change

Your spending pattern is likely different now.

Some expenses shrink after loss. Others — like healthcare, home maintenance, or support for children — may grow.

Understanding your real expenses helps you:

- Build a new, honest budget
- Reduce unnecessary stress
- Plan for short-term and long-term needs

### *Key Expenses to Review:*

- **Housing:** Mortgage/rent, utilities, property taxes, homeowners insurance
- **Healthcare:** Insurance premiums, out-of-pocket costs, medications
- **Transportation:** Car loans, gas, maintenance, insurance
- **Food and living:** Groceries, clothing, household supplies
- **Debt payments:** Mortgage, credit cards, loans
- **Personal care:** Therapy, self-care, subscriptions
- **Childcare or support for dependents (if applicable)**

### *Real-World Example: Mike's Expenses*

Mike assumed his expenses would be cut in half after losing his wife. But after tracking them for a month, he realized:

- Housing costs were the same.
- Groceries dropped only 20%.
- Healthcare costs rose, because he lost his wife's employer health insurance plan.

Honest tracking helped Mike reframe his financial needs realistically.

**Action Step:**

Track your expenses for 30 days — no pressure, just curiosity.

See where money is truly flowing.

## Step 5: Putting It All Together – Your Financial Snapshot

Once you know your assets, liabilities, income, and expenses, you can build a simple snapshot:

**Sample Inventory Worksheet**

**Assets** (What I Own):

- Checking Account: $__________
- Savings Account: $__________
- 401(k) or IRA: $__________
- Home Value: $__________
- Vehicle Value: $__________
- Other: $__________

**Liabilities** (What I Owe):

- Mortgage Balance: $__________
- Auto Loan Balance: $__________
- Credit Card Debt: $__________
- Other: $__________

**Income Sources** (What's Coming In):

- Social Security Survivor Benefits: $__________/month
- Pension Income: $__________/month
- Employment Income: $__________/month
- Rental or Other Income: $__________/month

**Expenses** (What's Going Out):

- Housing: $__________/month
- Healthcare: $__________/month
- Food & Groceries: $__________/month
- Transportation: $__________/month
- Debt Payments: $__________/month
- Other: $__________/month

## Closing Reflection: Inventory Is a Beginning, Not a Judgment

Taking inventory isn't about beating yourself up.

It's about setting yourself free.

When you know what you have, what you owe, and what you need, you move from fear to focus.

You move from survival to strategy.

You move from confusion to clarity.

No matter what your numbers look like right now —

they are only your **starting place.**

They are not your ending place.

You are not behind.

You are not broken.

You are building — with strength, with wisdom, and with the quiet, relentless power of love honoring itself through survival.

You are doing better than you think.

And your next chapter is just beginning.

## Next Steps After Taking Financial Inventory

Now that you have your full financial picture in front of you,

here's what to do next — calmly, steadily, wisely.

### 1. Celebrate

- Acknowledge the courage it took to face the numbers.
- Remind yourself: Knowledge is power. Fear fades when facts are clear.

## 2. Organize Your Documents

- Gather and safely store copies of account statements, titles, policies, and debt balances.
- Create a simple folder (paper or digital) labeled **"Financial Inventory – [Year]"**.

## 3. Prioritize Short-Term Needs

- Make sure you can cover essential monthly expenses first (housing, food, healthcare, transportation).
- Set aside some of your emergency savings if possible (even small amounts matter).

## 4. Meet with Trusted Professionals (If Needed)

- Estate attorney (to handle ownership changes, probate, wills).
- Financial advisor (to review investments, retirement plans, survivor benefits).
- CPA or tax advisor (to prepare for taxes related to inheritance, Social Security, or life insurance).

## 5. Review Debts and Payment Plans

- Identify any urgent debts that need attention.
- Set up payment plans or payoff strategies that fit your new cash flow.

## 6. Start Dreaming Again

- Think quietly about your next chapter.
- Write down one financial hope for the next year — something that reflects *your* new life and purpose.

## Closing Reflection:

Taking inventory was an act of bravery.
Taking action now is an act of love —
for your past, your future, and for the new life you are choosing to build.
You are not just surviving.
You are leading yourself forward —
with clarity, courage, and heart.

## Widower's Financial Roadmap Overview

*(Seeing the Big Picture After Taking Inventory)*

## Widower's Financial Roadmap: From Inventory to Independence

You've taken the courageous first step:
You've gathered your financial facts.
Now what?
Here's the bigger journey ahead —
a clear, calm roadmap to guide your rebuilding process.

### Step 1: Take Inventory

- List your assets, liabilities, income, and expenses.
- Build your full financial snapshot.
- See your new starting line clearly.

### Step 2: Stabilize Your Cash Flow

- Prioritize essential monthly expenses.
- Adjust spending if needed to fit new income realities.
- Build (or rebuild) your emergency fund — even small steps matter.

### Step 3: Protect Your Foundations

- Update wills, healthcare directives, and powers of attorney.
- Retitle assets and accounts properly.
- Review and update beneficiary designations.

### Step 4: Rebuild Your Financial Plan

- Adjust retirement goals based on new circumstances.
- Review insurance coverage (life, health, auto, home).
- Create or update an investment strategy that matches your new goals and risk tolerance.

### Step 5: Grow and Dream Again

- Explore new personal goals: travel, hobbies, education, giving back.
- Plan for legacy and estate considerations (for children, charities, loved ones).
- Move from surviving to thriving — with purpose, peace, and financial confidence.

## Closing Encouragement:

You are not "starting over."

You are **starting forward** —

carrying love, carrying wisdom, carrying hope into the life still ahead of you.

And you don't have to do it all at once.

You are allowed to walk this road one brave step at a time.

## Gentle Financial Journal Prompts

*(Reflecting Emotionally After Taking Inventory)*

## Financial Reflection Journal Prompts for Widowers

You've completed your financial inventory —

an act of quiet, enormous courage.

Now take a few moments to reflect.

Not on numbers, but on what they mean for you — and the life you are still living.

There are no right or wrong answers.

Only honest ones.

1. What surprised me most when I saw my full financial picture?

2. What am I most proud of financially — big or small?

3. What financial fears have eased after completing my inventory?

4. What new financial fears or worries showed up — and how might I face them gently?

5. What financial strength or wisdom did my spouse pass on to me — and how am I honoring it?

6. If I could write a letter to myself 12 months from now about my financial journey, what would it say?

7. What does "financial peace" look like for me now?

8. What financial dream — small or large — feels worth moving toward?

## Closing Reflection:

You are not just rebuilding finances.
You are rebuilding belief —
in yourself,
in your future,
in your right to live fully and freely.
Your financial healing is sacred work.
And you are doing it beautifully, step by step.

## Widower's Simple Financial Priorities List

*(What to Tackle First, Second, Third After Inventory)*

## Your Simple Financial Priorities List

Now that you've seen your full financial picture,
it's time to move — not with panic, not with pressure —
but with purpose.
Here's how to gently prioritize your next steps:

## Priority 1: Stabilize Your Daily Life

- Make sure your **basic monthly bills** (housing, food, insurance, transportation) are covered.
- Set up a **basic cash flow plan**: income vs expenses.
- Ensure you have **access to emergency cash** if needed.

## Priority 2: Protect Your Legal and Financial Foundation

- **Retitle** major assets into your name (bank accounts, home, car).
- **Update your will** and powers of attorney to reflect your new reality.
- **Review beneficiary designations** on all retirement accounts, life insurance policies, and investment accounts.

## Priority 3: Rebuild Your Safety Net

- Build or replenish an **emergency fund** (aim for 3–6 months of basic expenses over time).
- Review your **insurance coverage** (health, home, auto, and life).
- Consult a **CPA or tax advisor** about any new tax considerations.

## Priority 4: Plan for Long-Term Stability

- Meet with a **trusted financial advisor** to adjust your retirement or investment plan.
- Explore options for **managing or paying down debt** if needed.
- Begin setting **small financial goals** (saving for a trip, building savings, giving back).

## Closing Reminder:

You do not have to tackle everything at once.

Just take the next right step — one step at a time — and let your progress build.

You are moving toward security, dignity, and peace —
and you are doing it with strength and grace.

## After Inventory: What to Focus on Now

You've done the hard work of facing your finances.

You've built your financial snapshot.

You've taken ownership of your new starting line.

Now it's time to gently move forward.

But remember:

Forward doesn't mean **fast.**

Forward doesn't mean **perfect.**

Forward just means:

One strong, thoughtful step at a time.

In the next sections of this book, we will focus on:

- **Stabilizing your cash flow** so you can breathe easier month to month.
- **Protecting what you've rebuilt** through legal updates and smart insurance choices.
- **Planning for your future** with confidence — even if you are still grieving, even if you are still figuring things out.

You will learn how to:

- Create a sustainable budget for your new life
- Build emergency savings gradually
- Protect yourself from new risks
- Rebuild dreams you thought were out of reach

No matter how messy, scary, or uncertain this feels —
you are not broken.
You are building.
And you are allowed to build at your own pace, with your own heart, toward your own definition of peace and prosperity.
You are doing better than you think.
And you are not alone.
Let's keep walking forward — together.

## Financial Healing Affirmations

*(For Widowers — Gentle Reminders for the Journey)*

## Financial Healing Affirmations

Grief is not just emotional.
It's financial.
It's physical.
It's spiritual.
There will be days when facing money feels too heavy.
There will be days when the road ahead looks too long.
When that happens, return here.
Read these words slowly.
Let them remind you:
You are still healing.
You are still rebuilding.
And you are doing better than you think.

## I am allowed to move slowly.

Financial healing is not a race.

## I am allowed to ask questions.

Wisdom grows from curiosity, not from knowing everything upfront.

## I am allowed to make mistakes and correct them.

Every mistake is a stepping stone — not a life sentence.

## I am building something worth protecting.

Every dollar, every decision, every act of care is building my new foundation.

## I am honoring my past and protecting my future.

My financial strength honors the love and life I shared.

## I am allowed to dream again.

Survival was necessary.
Thriving is allowed.

## I have faced what many fear — and I am still standing.

That strength runs deeper than any number in any bank account.

## I deserve stability, peace, and dignity.

Financial security is not greed.
It's protection.
It's love for myself and those I care for.

## I am writing a new chapter — bravely, patiently, wisely.

This chapter is mine.
It is sacred.
It is unfolding, one steady step at a time.

## Closing Reflection:

Healing is not linear.
Neither is financial rebuilding.
But both are possible.
And both are already happening — inside you, one breath, one choice, one act of courage at a time.
You are not alone.

## And you are more powerful than you know.

## Your Top 5 Financial Focus Areas for the Next Year

You don't need 100 goals.
You don't need a complicated plan.
You just need **steady focus** —
on what will truly stabilize and strengthen your life for the long term.
Here are your top 5 areas to gently prioritize over the next year:

## 1. Secure Your Cash Flow

- Build a realistic monthly budget based on your new income and expenses.
- Make sure essentials (housing, food, healthcare) are covered first.

## 2. Strengthen Your Emergency Fund

- Aim for at least 3–6 months of essential expenses saved.
- Even small, steady deposits are powerful over time.

## 3. Update Your Legal and Beneficiary Documents

- Review and update your will, healthcare proxy, and financial powers of attorney.
- Update beneficiaries on retirement accounts, life insurance, and bank accounts.

## 4. Review Your Insurance Protection

- Ensure health, homeowners, auto, and life insurance policies meet your current needs.
- Adjust coverage as needed for affordability and risk management.

## 5. Rebuild Retirement and Investment Plans

- Meet with a financial advisor (if needed) to adjust your investment strategy.
- Create a basic retirement timeline — based on your new financial picture — to work toward steadily.

## Closing Encouragement:

If you focus on just these five areas,
you will be rebuilding a strong, resilient financial life.
You don't have to fix everything overnight.
You only have to keep moving forward, one wise, steady step at a time.
You are not just surviving this chapter.
You are preparing for a new one —
one filled with security, dignity, hope, and pride.

## 12-Month Financial Milestones Tracker

You don't have to do everything at once.
You just have to move forward — a little each month.
This tracker is here to remind you:
**Progress is still progress — even if it feels small, even if it feels slow.**
Use this to mark your milestones over the next year.

### Month 1

- Completed a full financial inventory (assets, liabilities, income, expenses).
- Set up a basic monthly budget.

### Month 2

- Verified access to all accounts (bank, investment, insurance).
- Paid all essential monthly bills with updated cash flow.

## Month 3

- Updated beneficiaries on retirement accounts and life insurance.
- Contacted Social Security (if applicable) to confirm benefits.

## Month 4

- Built or added to an emergency fund.
- Reviewed mortgage, rent, or housing costs for affordability.

## Month 5

- Scheduled a check-in meeting with a trusted financial advisor (if desired).
- Identified and prioritized any outstanding debts to tackle.

## Month 6

- Reviewed insurance coverage (health, home, auto, life).
- Began tracking spending habits more mindfully.

## Month 7

- Completed or updated a will, healthcare proxy, and financial power of attorney.
- Celebrated a small financial win (no matter how small).

## Month 8

- Reassessed short-term and long-term financial goals.
- Explored ways to automate bill payments or savings.

### Month 9

- Reviewed investments or retirement plans.
- Adjusted financial plans as needed for new goals or realities.

### Month 10

- Reflected on financial progress made so far.
- Paid off or reduced at least one outstanding debt or bill.

### Month 11

- Started a new financial habit (monthly check-ins, journaling wins, saving challenges).
- Planned for any year-end financial needs (charitable giving, tax preparation).

### Month 12

- Completed a full-year financial review.
- Set new goals and dreams for the next year ahead.

## Closing Reminder:

Each box you check is a celebration.
Each milestone you hit is proof of your strength.
Each step forward is a gift to your future self —
and to the life you are still courageously building.
You are doing better than you think.

## Widower's Financial Wins Journal

## My Financial Wins Journal

Grief focuses on what was lost.

This journal focuses on what is being **rebuilt**.

Every time you complete a financial task — no matter how small — record it here.

Every win is proof:

You are not standing still.

You are moving forward.

You are becoming financially stronger, wiser, and freer every day.

Date: ______________

**Today I accomplished:**

**How I feel about it:**

Date: ______________

**Today I accomplished:**

**How I feel about it:**

Date: ______________

**Today I accomplished:**

**How I feel about it:**

(Repeat as often as you want — there's no limit to the wins you can record.)

## Need inspiration for what counts as a win?

- Paid a bill on time.
- Called a bank or insurance company to update information.
- Said no to unnecessary spending.

- Asked a financial question you didn't know how to ask before.
- Saved $10 toward an emergency fund.
- Updated a will or beneficiary form.
- Walked away from a scam or high-pressure sales pitch.
- Made a new financial dream list.
- Talked with a trusted professional for advice.
- Gave yourself grace after a financial mistake.

**If it moved you forward, it counts.**

## Closing Reflection:

Healing doesn't just happen on the outside.
It happens deep inside —
where hope rebuilds, where wisdom roots, where new dreams are born.
Every win you record is a light on your path.
And you are lighting the way —
for yourself, for your family, for your future.
Keep going.
You are doing beautifully.

# Chapter 6: Bank Accounts, Credit Cards, and Debt

## Introduction: You've Carried Enough Weight — Let's Lighten It

Bank accounts.
Credit cards.
Loans.
Debt.
These words probably didn't used to feel so heavy.
Before loss, they were just another part of daily life.
But now, in the aftermath of losing your spouse, they can feel overwhelming —
like a tangled web you're supposed to somehow untangle while still grieving.
If you're feeling that way, take a deep breath.
You're not alone.
And you're not expected to "figure it all out" in a day.
This chapter will walk you through the financial steps surrounding accounts and debt,
gently and clearly,
so you can protect your future, lighten your load, and move forward with dignity.

You are already carrying enough.

Let's work together to make sure money isn't another unnecessary weight on your shoulders.

## Part 1: Handling Bank Accounts After Loss

One of the first practical tasks widowers face is sorting out bank accounts.

It can feel clinical and cruel — dealing with paperwork when you're still reeling emotionally.

But it's important — not just for legal reasons, but for your protection and peace of mind.

Let's start simple.

### *Step 1: Locate All Bank Accounts*

You need to know:

- Where your money is.
- Whose name is on each account.
- What access rules apply.

This includes:

- Checking accounts
- Savings accounts
- Money market accounts
- Certificates of deposit (CDs)

### *Step 2: Understand Types of Ownership*

Different accounts have different rules depending on how they were titled:

- **Joint Accounts with Right of Survivorship:**

- Automatically transfer to you without probate.
- You simply need to present a death certificate.
- **Individual Accounts in Spouse's Name Only:**
- May require probate court involvement unless other transfer-on-death arrangements were made.
- **Payable-on-Death (POD) Accounts:**
- Also transfer automatically to the named beneficiary (you) when you present proof of death.

### *Step 3: Retitle, Close, or Open New Accounts*

Depending on the situation, you'll need to:

- **Retitle joint accounts** into your name alone.
- **Close unnecessary accounts** that were solely in your spouse's name (after probate, if required).
- **Open a new personal account** if needed for clean record-keeping and emotional closure.

**Action Step:**

Make a simple chart listing every bank account, current status (joint/ind ividual/POD), and next steps needed.

## Part 2: Handling Credit Cards After Loss

Credit cards can cause confusion — and trouble — if not handled properly after a spouse's death.

Here's the good news:

You are **not automatically responsible** for your spouse's individual debts.

But shared debts are a different story.

Let's unpack this carefully.

### *Step 1: Identify the Type of Card*

- **Joint Credit Card Account:**
- You co-signed together.
- You are legally responsible for the balance.
- **Authorized User Credit Card:**
- You were simply authorized to use your spouse's card.
- Typically, you are **not** responsible for paying the debt unless you cosigned the account.
- **Spouse's Sole Account:**
- If the card was in your spouse's name alone and you weren't a joint applicant, the estate is responsible for the debt — not you personally.

### *Step 2: Notify the Credit Card Companies*

Contact each credit card company where your spouse had an account.
You'll typically need:

- A copy of the death certificate.
- Proof of your identity.
- Information about the estate (if relevant).

Ask:

- How they handle the account after death.
- Whether you are personally liable for the balance (get it in writing).

### *Step 3: Monitor Credit Reports*

You'll want to check your own credit report and, if allowed, your deceased spouse's credit report for:

- Outstanding debts

- Open accounts you may have forgotten
- Signs of identity theft

You can request free reports at **AnnualCreditReport.com**.

**Action Step:**

Create a list of every credit card account, the type (joint, authorized user, spouse-only), and action taken.

## Part 3: Protecting Your Credit After a Spouse's Death

You may not have thought much about your credit score before.

But now, it matters — because it protects your ability to:

- Rent or buy a home
- Refinance debt if needed
- Access favorable insurance rates
- Finance future purchases, if necessary

Here's how to gently safeguard your credit during this sensitive time:

### *1. Monitor Accounts Closely*

Keep an eye on bank and credit card statements for:

- Unauthorized charges
- Missed payments
- Overdrafts or errors

### *2. Pay Minimums if Necessary*

If money is tight, paying the **minimum required payments** protects your credit score better than letting accounts become delinquent.

Later, you can make bigger payments once you're stabilized.

### *3. Correct Errors Quickly*

If you see:

- Accounts incorrectly reported as delinquent
- Accounts still listing your deceased spouse's name
- Incorrect personal information

Dispute them in writing with the credit bureaus immediately.

**Action Step:**

Set a reminder once a month to check your credit report or statements for accuracy.

## Part 4: Managing or Eliminating Shared Debts

Debt after loss can feel suffocating.

You didn't choose this.

You didn't plan for this.

But you can take control of it — wisely, patiently, bravely.

### *Step 1: Know What You're Responsible For*

Only shared, cosigned debts are truly your personal responsibility.

Medical debts, loans, credit cards —

if your name is on it, it's yours.

If not, it typically falls to the estate.

### *Step 2: Prioritize Debts*

Start with:

- Essential secured debts (mortgage, auto loans)
- Then unsecured debts (credit cards, personal loans)

The goal is to protect your home, your transportation, and your credit standing first.

### *Step 3: Explore Repayment Options*

You have choices:

- **Pay debts off slowly** through regular monthly payments.
- **Negotiate settlements** for reduced payoff amounts (especially for credit cards or medical bills).
- **Use life insurance or other proceeds cautiously** — don't rush to pay off everything without a clear plan.

**Pros of Paying Debts Quickly:**

- Peace of mind
- Lower monthly expenses
- Stronger credit profile

**Cons of Paying Debts Quickly:**

- May drain cash reserves needed for emergencies
- May leave you cash-poor but "debt-free" in a risky way

**Action Step:**

Make a simple debt list by priority: What must be handled now? What can wait? What can be negotiated?

## Part 5: Should You Consolidate Debt?

Some widowers consider debt consolidation — combining multiple debts into one loan with a (hopefully) lower payment.

Is it a good idea?

Here's the honest truth:

**Pros of Consolidating Debt:**

- Simplified monthly payments (one instead of many)
- Potentially lower interest rates
- Easier to manage cash flow during emotional recovery

**Cons of Consolidating Debt:**

- You may pay more in total interest over time.
- Some consolidation loans come with hidden fees or penalties.
- You still need a solid budget — consolidation doesn't erase debt.

*When Consolidation Makes Sense:*

- You have good credit and qualify for a **low-interest personal loan**.
- You're feeling overwhelmed managing multiple bills.
- You can commit to not racking up new debt afterward.

*When Consolidation Doesn't Make Sense:*

- You have minimal debt that can be handled faster with small payments.
- You would incur high fees or penalties.
- You might be tempted to rack up new credit card balances again.

**Action Step:**

If considering consolidation, get three written loan offers and compare total costs — not just monthly payments.

## Real-World Example: David's Debt Decision

David was drowning in grief —
and three credit cards totaling $22,000 didn't help.
He thought about using life insurance money to pay them all off immediately.
Instead, he:

- Made minimum payments for the first 6 months to stabilize cash flow.
- Built a 4-month emergency fund first.
- Then paid off the smallest debt first for momentum ("snowball method").

Today, he is debt-free —
and emotionally stronger for having moved carefully, not reactively.
You have that strength too.

## Closing Reflection: Your Financial Life is Yours to Rebuild — Wisely, Slowly, Proudly

Bank accounts.
Credit cards.
Debt.
They aren't just numbers anymore.
They're part of the story you're writing:
the story of survival, strength, wisdom, and rebuilding.
You don't have to rush.
You don't have to fix everything in a month.
You just have to keep moving forward —
one wise, self-respecting decision at a time.
You are not just protecting your credit.
You are protecting your future.
You are protecting your peace.

And you are doing it beautifully.

## Bank and Credit Card Accounts After Loss Checklist

You don't have to handle everything in a day.

But step by step, you can take back control of your financial life — starting here.

### Step 1: Locate All Accounts

- Find all checking, savings, money market, and investment accounts.
- Find all credit cards, store cards, and lines of credit.

### Step 2: Gather Essential Information

- Account numbers.
- Names listed on the account (joint, individual, authorized user).
- Outstanding balances (for credit cards or lines of credit).

### Step 3: Notify Banks and Credit Card Companies

- Provide a death certificate (official or certified copy).
- Ask about survivorship rights (for joint accounts).
- Ask about account closure or retitling process (for solo accounts).
- Ask how debts will be handled (for credit cards).

### Step 4: Retitle or Open New Accounts

- Retitle joint bank accounts into your name alone.
- Open new personal accounts if needed for simplicity and security.

### Step 5: Monitor Accounts

- Watch for unusual activity (fraud protection).
- Update automatic payments or direct deposits to your new accounts.

### Step 6: Review Your Credit Reports

- Order your free credit reports at AnnualCreditReport.com.
- Correct any errors or outdated information.

## Closing Reminder:

Every account you retitle, every bill you update, every small step you take —

it's a signal to yourself and to the world:
You are still standing.
You are still leading your life forward.
You are stronger than you feel.

## Debt Decision-Making Worksheet

*(For Widowers — Calm, Clear, Empowering)*

## My Debt Decision-Making Worksheet

You don't have to panic about debt.

You just need a clear plan — one that honors your peace, your goals, and your dignity.

Use this worksheet to decide your next steps calmly.

## Step 1: List Your Debts

Type of Debt Balance Owed Minimum Payment Joint / Solo Notes

Mortgage

$____________

$______________

Joint/Solo

Auto Loan

$____________

$______________

Joint/Solo

Credit Card 1

$____________

$______________

Joint/Solo

Credit Card 2

$____________

$______________

Joint/Solo

Personal Loan

$____________

$______________

Joint/Solo

Medical Bills

$____________

$______________

Joint/Solo

## Step 2: Identify Priority Debts

- Secured debts (home, car) usually come first.
- Essential debts (healthcare-related) come next.
- Unsecured debts (credit cards, personal loans) come after.

### Step 3: Evaluate Your Payment Options

For each debt, ask:

- Can I afford to continue minimum monthly payments comfortably?
- Do I have savings to pay this off safely — **without** draining my emergency fund?
- Would consolidating or negotiating this debt help me or hurt me financially?

### Step 4: Choose Your Strategy

Debt Type Strategy (Circle One)
Mortgage
Continue / Refinance / Sell
Auto Loan
Continue / Refinance / Sell
Credit Card 1
Continue / Pay Off / Settle / Consolidate
Credit Card 2
Continue / Pay Off / Settle / Consolidate
Personal Loan
Continue / Pay Off / Settle / Consolidate
Medical Bills
Continue / Negotiate / Settle

### Step 5: Make a Gentle Plan

- List the first debt you want to tackle.
- Set a target date or milestone (example: "Pay off Credit Card 2 within 12 months").
- Allow flexibility — healing and rebuilding are not rigid processes.

## Closing Reflection:

Debt is not a reflection of your worth.

It's a puzzle to solve with wisdom and patience.

You are not broken because you carry debt.

You are brave because you are carrying it with clarity, with dignity, and with a plan.

You are doing better than you think.

## Debt Snowball vs Debt Avalanche

*(Choosing Your Debt Payoff Strategy)*

## Choosing Your Debt Payoff Strategy: Snowball vs Avalanche

Once you know what debts you have, the next question is:

**How should I start paying them off?**

There's no perfect answer — only what fits your situation best.

Here are two common, proven strategies explained simply:

### 1. The Debt Snowball Method

**How it works:**

- List all your debts from smallest balance to largest balance.
- Pay minimum payments on all debts except the smallest.
- Focus all extra money on paying off the smallest debt first.
- Once that's paid, roll the money into the next smallest debt — and so on.

**Why it works emotionally:**

- You see quick wins early.
- Each debt you eliminate builds momentum and confidence.
- It feels like you're gaining control faster.

**Pros:**

- Builds positive motivation quickly.
- Helps you feel emotionally stronger after every win.
- Keeps you mentally engaged during the healing journey.

**Cons:**

- You might pay slightly more in interest overall compared to Avalanche.

**Snowball is great for widowers who:**

- Need fast emotional wins to stay motivated.
- Feel overwhelmed and need to simplify progress.
- Prefer momentum over pure math.

## 2. The Debt Avalanche Method

**How it works:**

- List all your debts from highest interest rate to lowest interest rate.
- Pay minimums on all debts except the one with the highest rate.
- Focus all extra money on paying down the most expensive debt first.

**Why it works mathematically:**

- You save more money on interest over time.
- You pay off your total debt faster — even if early wins are slower.

**Pros:**

- Reduces total interest paid.
- Gets rid of the "most expensive" debt first.

**Cons:**

- Progress may feel slower emotionally.
- Takes longer to "check off" a first victory.

**Avalanche is great for widowers who:**

- Feel emotionally strong enough to stay focused even if it takes time.
- Want to minimize long-term interest costs.
- Prefer math-driven results.

## Which One Should You Pick?

The honest truth:

**The best method is the one you will stick with.**

There is no "wrong" choice.

There is only *forward.*

You can even blend both:

- Start with a Snowball for emotional wins.
- Switch to Avalanche once you gain momentum.

The goal is not perfection.

The goal is freedom — emotionally and financially.

And you are getting closer every day.

# Financial Rebuilding Timeline Overview

*(Mapping the Journey After Loss)*

## Your Financial Rebuilding Timeline: A Gentle Overview

Rebuilding after loss isn't a checklist.

It's a journey.

And just like grief, it's not perfectly linear.

It twists, turns, pauses, and restarts.

But there is a flow —

a steady path you can follow, one phase at a time.

Here's what the rebuilding process often looks like:

### Phase 1: Stabilization (First 0–6 Months)

- Take a financial inventory (assets, liabilities, income, expenses).
- Set up access to all bank accounts and close or retitle old ones.
- Handle immediate debt management (minimum payments to protect credit).
- Monitor accounts for fraud or identity theft.
- Focus on emotional and financial survival, not perfection.

### Phase 2: Protection (6–12 Months)

- Update your will, healthcare directives, and powers of attorney.
- Update beneficiaries on all accounts (bank, investment, insurance).
- Build (or rebuild) an emergency fund (even \$500–\$1,000 matters).
- Review and adjust insurance coverage as needed.
- Make a basic new budget reflecting your life now.

### Phase 3: Strengthening (12–24 Months)

- Choose a debt payoff strategy (Snowball, Avalanche, or blended).
- Increase retirement savings contributions if possible.
- Review investment accounts and long-term plans with a trusted advisor.
- Begin dreaming again — set personal and financial goals for the future.

### Phase 4: Growth (24 Months and Beyond)

- Fine-tune a full financial plan: retirement, estate planning, giving.
- Explore travel, hobbies, education, or charitable work that honors your next chapter.
- Build legacy plans if desired (trusts, letters to family, charitable gifts).
- Live with dignity, freedom, stability — and pride in the life you are rebuilding.

## Closing Reflection:

Your timeline is **yours** —
not the world's, not society's, not anyone else's.
You are not behind.
You are not late.
You are right on time —
for the life still unfolding,
for the strength still growing inside you,
for the future still waiting to be built.
One strong, self-respecting step at a time.

# Chapter 7: Updating Beneficiaries and Legal Documents

## Introduction: Why This Matters So Much

Some parts of loss feel obvious:

the absence at the dinner table, the quietness of the house, the empty side of the bed.

Other parts — like updating legal documents — feel almost invisible.

Not urgent.

Not emotional.

Easier to ignore.

But here's the truth:

**Failing to update your beneficiaries and legal documents after losing your spouse can create real financial disasters down the road — for you, for your children, for the people you love.**

You don't have to do everything today.

You don't have to rush.

But you do have to move steadily.

Because protecting your future now is one of the greatest acts of self-respect — and love for the family and future still around you.

This chapter will walk you through it.

Gently.

Clearly.

Confidently.

Let's start where you are.

## Part 1: Why Updating Beneficiaries and Legal Documents Is Urgent

There are two reasons this needs your attention now — not years from now.

### *1. Beneficiary Designations Override Wills*

Many people believe their will controls who inherits their assets.

But here's the truth:

- Life insurance policies
- Retirement accounts (401(k), IRA)
- Transfer-on-death accounts at banks
- Annuities
- Some investment accounts

**All pass according to the beneficiary form you signed — NOT your will.**

That means:

- Even if you update your will, if your spouse is still listed on your retirement account or life insurance policy, the money will still go to them.
- If your spouse is gone, and no new beneficiary is named, your account could get stuck in probate — a long, stressful, costly legal process for your family.

### *2. You Need to Appoint New Decision-Makers*

Your spouse was likely named:

- Your healthcare power of attorney (to make medical decisions if you couldn't)
- Your financial power of attorney (to handle money decisions if you became incapacitated)
- Your executor (the person in charge of carrying out your will)

Without your spouse, there's now a gap.

Someone trustworthy needs to be legally appointed to these roles — or the court may choose someone for you.

And you deserve better than that.

## Part 2: What Needs to Be Updated

Let's go through it step-by-step — calmly, clearly, simply.

You don't have to do everything at once.

But you *do* need a list.

### *1. Retirement Accounts*

- 401(k)s
- 403(b)s
- Traditional IRAs
- Roth IRAs
- Pension plans

**Action Step:**

Contact the plan administrator or financial institution and ask:

- Who is currently listed as my beneficiary?

- How can I update my beneficiary designation?

Often you can change beneficiaries online or with a simple form.
Choose:

- A primary beneficiary (first in line to receive assets)
- A contingent beneficiary (backup in case the primary beneficiary has passed)

### *2. Life Insurance Policies*

- Group life insurance through your employer
- Private life insurance policies
- Annuity contracts with death benefits

**Action Step:**
Request a "Change of Beneficiary" form from each insurer.
Remember:
Beneficiary forms override wills — no matter what your intentions are.

### *3. Bank and Investment Accounts*

- Bank accounts with Payable on Death (POD) designations
- Investment accounts with Transfer on Death (TOD) designations

**Action Step:**
Visit the bank or brokerage.
Update the names on file for your POD/TOD designations.

### *4. Legal Documents*

- **Last Will and Testament:** Who inherits your property?
- **Living Will (Advance Healthcare Directive):** Your medical wishes if incapacitated.
- **Durable Financial Power of Attorney:** Who can handle your financial affairs if you can't?
- **Healthcare Power of Attorney:** Who can make healthcare decisions on your behalf?
- **Trust documents (if you have a trust):** Update successor trustees and beneficiaries.

**Real-World Example: Paul's Story**

Paul never updated his IRA after losing his wife.

When he died years later, the account had no living beneficiary.

It was forced through probate, delaying inheritance for his kids by nearly a year — and costing thousands in legal fees.

He didn't mean for that to happen.

He just didn't know.

You now know.

And that knowledge is power — quiet, healing, life-changing power.

## Part 3: How to Work with an Estate Attorney or Financial Planner

You don't have to figure everything out alone.

In fact, sometimes trying to "DIY" your estate updates after a major life change can cause more harm than good.

Here's when — and how — to seek professional help.

### *Why an Estate Attorney Can Help*

An estate attorney can:

- Review your existing documents to identify gaps.
- Help you create or update a will, living will, and powers of attorney.
- Help you set up trusts if needed for minor children, blended families, or charitable goals.
- Make sure your plans follow your state's specific legal rules.

### *Why a Financial Planner Can Help*

A financial planner can:

- Review all your assets and account titles.
- Help you adjust your retirement plans based on your new goals.
- Help you rebalance investments if your risk tolerance has changed.
- Coordinate with your estate attorney for comprehensive planning.

**How to Find Good Help:**

- Ask trusted friends or family for recommendations.
- Search for fee-only fiduciary financial planners (they are legally required to act in your best interest).
- Interview estate attorneys and planners — choose someone who listens more than they talk.

**What to Bring to Your First Meeting:**

- Copies of your old will, powers of attorney, and trust documents.
- List of all financial accounts and policies.
- Recent statements for retirement accounts, life insurance, bank accounts.

- Death certificate of your spouse.

**Real-World Example: James's Story**

James thought he didn't need to update anything after his wife died.

But when he remarried six years later and wanted to make sure his grown children still inherited part of his estate, he discovered:

- His wife was still named on two retirement accounts.
- His will didn't mention his new marriage.
- His powers of attorney were outdated.

Working with an estate attorney saved his family massive confusion and conflict — and gave James peace.

## Part 4: Emotional Barriers — and How to Overcome Them

Updating legal documents after loss doesn't just feel boring.

It can feel like betrayal.

Like you're erasing your spouse's place in your life.

You're not.

You are **honoring** their love by protecting yourself.

You are **carrying forward** their legacy by ensuring your life — and your family's future — is secure, dignified, and cared for.

It's okay to cry while doing paperwork.

It's okay to feel anger, sadness, or guilt.

You don't have to pretend this is easy.

You just have to keep moving forward — one loving act at a time.

## Closing Reflection: You Are Rebuilding Your Life — One Protected Step at a Time

Every form you fill out.

Every beneficiary you update.

Every legal gap you close.

It's not just paperwork.

It's an act of love.

An act of survival.

An act of honoring the past and protecting the future.

You are not erasing your spouse by moving forward.

You are carrying their love with you — into a new season of wisdom, strength, and leadership over your own life.

You are doing better than you think.

You are standing taller than you realize.

You are not just surviving.

You are rebuilding — wisely, steadily, proudly.

And your best days are still ahead.

# Part 3: Managing Income, Spending, and Saving

After the initial storm of loss, a new question quietly emerges:

**How do I live, day to day, with what I have now?**

Part 3 of this book is about answering that question.

Not with pressure.

Not with unrealistic goals.

But with real, steady tools that allow you to manage your money — and your life — with greater peace, control, and dignity.

This section is where short-term survival begins to transform into long-term stability.

We'll walk you through:

- Understanding your new income sources, whether it's Social Security survivor benefits, pensions, employment, or retirement withdrawals.
- Creating a realistic monthly budget that reflects your life today — not your life before loss.
- Adjusting spending habits to fit your new cash flow — without guilt, shame, or fear.
- Building (or rebuilding) your savings safety nets — emergency funds, short-term savings, and long-term retirement planning.
- Setting up simple systems to track, automate, and protect your money, even if you've never done it before.

- Making decisions about major expenses with thoughtfulness rather than impulse or grief-driven emotion.
- Planning ahead for irregular expenses — taxes, healthcare costs, home repairs — so you're never caught off guard.

Throughout Part 3, we'll treat your financial life as part of your overall healing process —

not something separate, not something you're expected to "master" overnight.

You'll learn how to:

- Prioritize needs over wants — without feeling like you're living in constant deprivation.
- Handle big financial decisions slowly and wisely.
- Protect your financial confidence by building small, repeatable wins.
- Trust yourself again when it comes to money.

By the end of Part 3, you'll have a working financial system that gives you room to breathe —

not just enough to get by, but enough to begin imagining what life could look like beyond mere survival.

This section is about claiming your right to security, stability, and yes — even hope —

through the steady, quiet power of smart financial stewardship.

You are not rebuilding a house of cards.

You are laying the bricks of a strong, resilient future —

one thoughtful decision, one paycheck, one savings deposit at a time.

And you are not alone.

# Chapter 8: Creating a New Budget

## Introduction: Your New Life Deserves a New Plan

When your spouse died, your entire world shifted.

It wasn't just the obvious parts — the conversations, the routines, the companionship.

It was the invisible parts too:

The way bills got paid.

The way money came in and went out.

The unspoken financial rhythm of your shared life.

Now, everything feels different.

And trying to live by the same old financial blueprint feels like trying to walk around in clothes that no longer fit.

**That's not failure.**

It's reality.

And it's why you need a **new budget** — one built for the life you are living today, not the life you had yesterday.

You're not "starting over."

You're starting forward.

And this chapter will walk you through it — one clear, steady step at a time.

## Part 1: Why Old Budgets Don't Fit New Lives

Before we talk about numbers, let's talk about grief.

Grief changes everything —
not just emotionally, but financially.
You might be facing:

- A reduced household income
- Higher healthcare costs
- Different housing needs
- New responsibilities for dependents
- A need for greater flexibility in how you spend your time and money

Trying to stick to your old budget after a major loss is like trying to use an old map for a new city.

You'll get lost.

You'll get frustrated.

And you'll feel like something's wrong with you — when really, the problem is that the map no longer matches the terrain.

**Permission:**

You are allowed to let go of your old budget.

You are allowed to build a new one that fits the reality of your life today.

And you don't have to figure it all out at once.

## Part 2: How to Track Expenses When You're Grieving

In theory, budgeting sounds simple:

- Add up your income.
- Add up your expenses.
- Make sure your expenses are less than your income.

But grief complicates everything.

Focus is harder.

Decisions feel heavier.

Paperwork feels unbearable some days.

So we need a grief-aware approach to tracking expenses — one that honors where you are emotionally while still helping you move forward.

### *Step 1: Give Yourself Permission to Be Imperfect*

You're not going to track every penny right away.

You're not going to create the "perfect" spreadsheet overnight.

That's okay.

The goal is progress, not perfection.

### *Step 2: Pick One Simple Tracking Method*

Choose something manageable:

- A small notebook where you jot down major expenses once a week.
- A basic Excel or Google Sheets spreadsheet.
- A simple budgeting app like Mint, YNAB (You Need A Budget), or EveryDollar.

**Pick the tool you'll actually use, not the one that sounds fancy.**

### *Step 3: Start with What You Know*

You don't have to backtrack through every receipt or bill from the past six months.

Start with:

- Current monthly bills (housing, utilities, insurance, car payments)
- Recent grocery shopping totals
- Any regular debts or obligations

Capture the "big rocks" first.
You can refine later.

### *Step 4: Track for 30 Days, No Judgment*

For one month:

- Track where your money actually goes.
- Notice patterns.
- Don't beat yourself up.

You're gathering information, not grading yourself.

## Part 3: Setting Realistic New Financial Goals

Once you have a sense of your current financial reality, it's time to set some new goals —

**but gently.**
Grief brain is real.
It's harder to plan long-term when you're still healing emotionally.
That's normal.
So we start small, realistic, and flexible.

### *Types of Financial Goals Widowers Commonly Set:*

- **Short-Term (0–12 months):**
- Cover all basic monthly expenses.
- Build or replenish an emergency fund.
- Pay down small debts if feasible.
- **Mid-Term (1–5 years):**
- Save for major home repairs or a reliable vehicle.
- Plan for upcoming life events (children's education, relocation, retirement).

- **Long-Term (5+ years):**
- Retire with dignity.
- Leave a financial legacy if desired.
- Give back to causes or people important to you.

### *Rules for Setting Realistic Goals:*

- Focus on **one or two priorities** at a time.
- Choose goals that are **measurable** (e.g., "Save $1,000 for emergencies" vs. "Save money").
- Allow your goals to change as your life changes.

**Real-World Example: Michael's New Goals**

Michael lost his wife at 62.
Before her death, they planned to travel extensively in retirement.
Now, his first financial goals were:

- Cover monthly bills without using credit cards.
- Save $5,000 in an emergency fund.
- Downsize to a smaller home within two years.

His dreams changed —
but his life didn't have to shrink.
It just had to evolve.

## Part 4: Understanding Essential Expenses vs. Discretionary Spending

When life changes suddenly, so must your spending priorities.

The first step in building a workable new budget is learning to distinguish between:

- **Essential Expenses:** Things you absolutely need to survive and stay stable.
- **Discretionary Expenses:** Things you want, enjoy, or could live without if necessary.

### *Examples of Essential Expenses:*

- Mortgage or rent
- Property taxes and insurance
- Utilities (gas, electricity, water, internet)
- Basic groceries
- Healthcare and health insurance
- Transportation (car payment, insurance, fuel)
- Minimum debt payments

### *Examples of Discretionary Expenses:*

- Dining out
- Entertainment subscriptions (Netflix, Spotify, etc.)
- Travel and vacations
- Gifts
- Hobbies (golf, photography, sports)
- Non-essential shopping (clothing, electronics)

**Reality Check:**

You don't have to eliminate all discretionary spending to be "responsible."

You just have to make sure essential needs come first —
and that discretionary spending fits your real income, not your old life's income.

**Action Step:**
On a piece of paper, draw two columns: "Essential" and "Discretionary."
List every monthly expense under the correct category.
This will give you incredible clarity.

## Part 5: Building a Gentle, Practical New Budget

You now have:

- A sense of your income
- A list of your expenses
- An understanding of essentials vs wants

Now, let's build your new budget.

### *Step 1: Calculate Monthly Income*

Total all sources:

- Social Security survivor benefits
- Pensions
- Retirement withdrawals
- Employment income
- Rental income
- Any other reliable sources

### *Step 2: Total Essential Expenses*

Add up all essentials.

- Housing
- Food
- Healthcare
- Transportation
- Minimum debt payments

If essentials exceed your income, we'll talk shortly about adjusting.

### *Step 3: Allocate for Discretionary Spending*

After essentials, set a **realistic** amount for discretionary spending.

- It's okay to leave room for joy.
- Just make sure it fits your real cash flow.

### *Step 4: Plan for Savings*

Even small amounts matter:

- Emergency fund
- Short-term goals
- Long-term retirement savings

Pay yourself first if possible — even if it's just $20/month at the start.

**Real-World Example: David's New Budget**

David lost his wife at 67.

Their dual Social Security checks had covered a comfortable lifestyle.

Now, with only one check, he built a budget focused on:

- Covering essentials first
- Reducing discretionary spending by 30%
- Saving $50/month into a rainy-day fund

It wasn't fancy.

It wasn't perfect.

But it worked.

And it gave him breathing room to grieve — and live — without constant financial fear.

## Part 6: Common Challenges — and How to Overcome Them

**Challenge 1:** Unexpected Expenses

**Solution:** Build a small emergency fund as quickly as possible. Even $500 can prevent disaster.

**Challenge 2:** Guilt About Spending on Yourself

**Solution:** Remember: Self-care spending (books, hobbies, simple joys) is not selfish. It's survival.

**Challenge 3:** Budget Fatigue

**Solution:** Review and refresh your budget every 90 days. Life changes — your budget should too.

**Challenge 4:** Inconsistent Income

**Solution:** Base your budget on your "bare minimum" income, not best-case scenarios. Flexibility is key.

## Closing Reflection: Your Budget Is a Promise — Not a Prison

A budget isn't punishment.

It isn't deprivation.

It's a promise you make —
to yourself,
to your future,
to the life you still have to live.

It's not about shrinking your dreams.
It's about protecting your right to dream again, safely and proudly.
You deserve to live without constant money fear.
You deserve financial peace.
And you are fully capable of building it —
one honest dollar, one wise decision, one brave month at a time.
Your new life deserves a new plan.
And you are writing it beautifully.

# Chapter 9: Rebuilding an Emergency Fund

## Introduction: Why Your Safety Net Matters Even More Now

Before loss, you might have felt like you had a built-in safety net.

A partner to lean on.

Two incomes.

Two sets of hands, two sets of eyes, two minds solving problems together.

After loss, that dynamic shifts overnight.

You are now the safety net —

for yourself, for your family, for your future.

And while that reality can feel heavy, it also points to something incredibly empowering:

You have the power to protect yourself.

You have the ability to build security, even in uncertain times.

At the heart of that security is something simple, powerful, and absolutely essential:

**Your emergency fund.**

This chapter will guide you through how to rebuild it —

calmly, steadily, wisely.

Because your financial safety is no longer just a nice-to-have.

It is your foundation.

And you deserve a strong one.

## Part 1: Why Your Emergency Fund Is More Important Than Ever

When you're grieving, money problems aren't just stressful.

They can be devastating.

One unexpected expense — a car repair, a medical bill, a leaky roof — can feel like the last straw when you're already stretched emotionally and financially thin.

An emergency fund protects you in ways that go far beyond money:

- It protects your peace of mind.
- It protects your healing.
- It protects your ability to say "no" to bad financial decisions made out of desperation.

**Real-World Example: Steven's Story**

Steven lost his wife when he was 55.

A few months later, his car needed $2,800 in urgent repairs.

Because they hadn't built an emergency fund together, Steven had to put the repair on a credit card — and watched helplessly as interest piled up, making grief feel even heavier.

Today, Steven shares his story so others understand:

**An emergency fund isn't about expecting the worst.**

**It's about refusing to be caught helpless when life happens.**

## Part 2: How Much Should You Aim For?

There's no one-size-fits-all number.

The right emergency fund depends on:

- Your current income sources
- Your monthly expenses
- Your responsibilities (kids, mortgage, medical needs)

- Your personal comfort level

### *Standard Guidelines:*

- **Starting Goal:** $1,000 to cover immediate minor emergencies.
- **Next Step Goal:** 3 months' worth of essential expenses.
- **Long-Term Goal:** 6–12 months' worth of essential expenses.

**What Counts as Essential Expenses?**

- Housing (mortgage/rent, utilities, insurance)
- Healthcare (insurance premiums, medications)
- Food
- Transportation
- Minimum debt payments

### *How to Calculate Your Personal Emergency Fund Target:*

Step 1:

Add up your essential monthly expenses.

Step 2:

Multiply that number by 3 (for a 3-month fund) or by 6 (for a 6-month fund).

Example:

If your essential expenses are $3,000 per month,

your 3-month emergency fund goal would be $9,000.

**Gentle Reminder:**

You don't have to get there tomorrow.

You just have to start.

Small, steady steps build powerful safety nets over time.

## Part 3: Where to Keep Your Emergency Fund

An emergency fund needs three key qualities:

- **Accessible:** You can get to it quickly when needed.
- **Safe:** It won't lose value because of market swings.
- **Separate:** It's not mixed in with your daily spending money.

### *Best Places to Keep an Emergency Fund:*

- **High-Yield Savings Accounts:**
- Online banks often offer better interest rates.
- Easy access while still earning some growth.
- **Money Market Accounts:**
- Similar to savings accounts but may offer higher rates and check-writing access.
- **Certificates of Deposit (CDs) Ladder:**
- Only for part of your fund.
- Create a ladder with different maturity dates for partial access.

### *Places to Avoid Storing Your Emergency Fund:*

- **Checking account you use daily:** Too easy to spend.
- **Investment accounts (stocks, bonds):** Too volatile. Value could drop when you need it most.
- **Physical cash at home:** Risky for theft, loss, and no growth.

**Action Step:**

Open a separate savings account specifically for your emergency fund.

Label it something meaningful, like "Peace of Mind Fund" or "Security Account."

Psychology matters.

Names matter.

## Part 4: Building (or Rebuilding) Your Emergency Fund from Scratch

If you're starting from zero (or close to it), you are not alone.

And you are not behind.

You are building — not just money, but strength.

Here's how to do it practically and compassionately.

### *Step 1: Set Your First Milestone*

Forget about 6 months' worth of expenses for now.

Aim first for $500 or $1,000.

That alone can prevent most common financial emergencies from spiraling.

### *Step 2: Create a Consistent Contribution Plan*

Even small automatic transfers add up over time:

- $20 per week = $1,040 per year
- $50 per week = $2,600 per year
- $100 per week = $5,200 per year

Set up automatic transfers from checking to savings.

Let the system work while you heal.

### *Step 3: Use "Found Money" to Boost It*

When you get unexpected cash:

- Tax refunds
- Birthday gifts
- Rebates

- Bonuses

Channel a portion of it into your emergency fund.

### *Step 4: Protect the Fund*

Only use it for **true emergencies**:

- Medical emergencies
- Home repairs that affect safety or health
- Car repairs essential for transportation
- Essential travel for family emergencies

Not for:

- Vacation expenses
- Holiday shopping
- Upgrading appliances that still work

**Real-World Example: Ben's Story**

Ben lost his wife and found himself overwhelmed with bills and grief.

He started his emergency fund with just $50 a month — less than what he used to spend on coffee and lunches out.

After a year, he had nearly $800 saved.

And when his furnace died in the winter, he didn't panic.

He simply used part of his emergency fund — and stayed warm and financially steady.

Small steps.

Big difference.

## Part 5: Pros and Cons of Different Emergency Fund Strategies

No strategy is perfect.

Each has trade-offs.

Let's walk through them honestly.

**High-Yield Savings Account**

Pros:

- Easy access
- Safe from market risks
- Earns more interest than checking

Cons:

- Tempting to dip into if not disciplined

**Money Market Account**

Pros:

- Higher interest rates than regular savings
- Check-writing and debit access in true emergencies

Cons:

- Minimum balance requirements sometimes apply

**CD Ladder**

Pros:

- Slightly higher returns
- Structured access at set intervals

Cons:

- Penalties for early withdrawal if you need funds urgently

**Physical Cash at Home**

Pros:

- Immediate access during emergencies (natural disasters, power outages)

Cons:

- No growth
- Risk of theft, fire, loss

**Action Step:**

Choose the strategy — or blend of strategies — that feels safest and most comfortable for you emotionally.

Safety isn't just about numbers.

It's about how your choices make you feel.

## Part 6: Emotional Barriers to Building an Emergency Fund — and How to Overcome Them

Building financial security after loss isn't just a math problem.

It's an emotional journey.

Here are common emotional hurdles widowers face — and how to gently move past them.

**Barrier 1: "I Can't Think That Far Ahead Right Now"**

Solution:

Just think about this week.

This month.

One tiny step at a time.

**Barrier 2: "I'll Never Be Able to Save Enough"**

Solution:

You don't have to hit the finish line today.

Small deposits count.

Momentum matters more than size.

**Barrier 3: "I Feel Guilty Saving When There's So Much I've Lost"**

Solution:

Building security honors what you lost — and honors the life you are still living.

Saving is an act of survival, not betrayal.

**Barrier 4: "What's the Point?"**

Solution:

The point is dignity.

The point is choice.

The point is peace.

You are worth protecting.

## Closing Reflection: Your Emergency Fund Is Your Quiet Superpower

You don't need a cape.

You don't need magic.

You already have everything you need to rebuild your safety net:

- Courage
- Wisdom
- Persistence
- Love for the life you are still building

Every dollar you save is a vote for your own future.

Every small transfer is an act of fierce self-respect.

Your emergency fund isn't just financial.

It's emotional armor.

It's the foundation of your next chapter.

And brick by brick, choice by choice, dollar by dollar —

you are already rebuilding something strong, sacred, and real.

# Chapter 10: Taxes for Widowers

## Introduction: Taxes Are Different After Loss — But You Can Handle This

If you're like most people, you probably never loved doing taxes even when life was "normal."

And now, after the death of your spouse, taxes can feel even more overwhelming:

- New forms
- New rules
- New questions you didn't even know to ask

It can feel unfair, complicated, and exhausting —

especially when your mind and heart are already carrying so much.

But here's the truth:

**You can handle this.**

You don't have to know everything overnight.

You don't have to become a tax expert.

You just need to know the basics — and know when to ask for help.

This chapter will walk you through the key tax issues widowers face: gently, clearly, and calmly.

By the end, you'll understand enough to file your taxes with more confidence —

and more importantly, you'll protect your future and your peace.

Let's start simple.

## Part 1: Filing Status the Year Your Spouse Dies

First, let's talk about your **filing status** — the single biggest factor that affects how much tax you'll owe.

The IRS allows special rules for widowers in the year your spouse dies.

Here's how it works:

### *If Your Spouse Died This Year:*

You can still **file jointly** for the year your spouse died — even if they passed away on January 1st or December 31st.

- You must have been legally married.
- You must not have remarried by December 31st.

**Why this matters:**

- Filing jointly usually gives you a higher standard deduction.
- Filing jointly often results in lower taxes owed than filing as a single person.

**Real-World Example: Alan's Story**

Alan's wife passed away in March.

Even though he lived most of the year alone, for tax purposes he filed as **Married Filing Jointly** for that tax year.

This saved him over $2,000 compared to filing as a Single filer.

You are allowed to take advantage of this.

It's not a loophole.

It's the law — designed to recognize that your household didn't instantly change financially just because your spouse passed early in the year.

**Important:**
When filing jointly for the year of death, you'll need:

- Your spouse's income documents (W-2s, 1099s, etc.)
- Proof of death (for Social Security benefits reporting, if relevant)
- Permission to sign on your spouse's behalf (the IRS allows this for a final joint return)

## Part 2: Qualifying Widow(er) Status

After the year your spouse dies, your filing status will likely change — but you might not have to file as "Single" right away.
There's a special, often-overlooked filing status:
**Qualifying Widow(er) with Dependent Child.**

### *Who Qualifies:*

- Your spouse died in one of the two previous years.
- You have a dependent child living with you.
- You paid more than half the cost of keeping up a home.

**Benefits of Qualifying Widow(er) Status:**

- You can use the **Married Filing Jointly** tax rates (lower taxes).
- You get a **higher standard deduction**.
- You have more time to adjust financially before filing as "Single."

**Real-World Example: Mark's Story**
Mark's wife passed away last year.
He's raising their 14-year-old daughter alone.
Mark qualified to file as a **Qualifying Widower** this year,
which saved him thousands in taxes and gave him precious breathing room during an already difficult time.

If you're raising a dependent child, this special status exists to protect you —
emotionally and financially.

### *How Long Can You Use It?*

- You can file as a Qualifying Widow(er) for **up to two tax years** following your spouse's death.
- After that, you must file as Single or Head of Household (depending on your situation).

## Part 3: Estate Taxes and Inheritance Taxes (Simplified)

When you hear "estate tax" or "inheritance tax," your first reaction might be fear.

Let's break it down calmly.

### *Federal Estate Tax*

The federal government only taxes very large estates.

In 2024, for example, an estate must be worth more than **$13.61 million** before it owes federal estate tax.

**Translation:**

- Most widowers will never owe federal estate taxes.
- If your spouse's estate was under that amount, you're safe from federal estate taxes.

### *State Estate Taxes and Inheritance Taxes*

Some states have their own estate or inheritance taxes — with much lower thresholds.

Examples:

- Maryland
- Massachusetts
- New York
- Oregon
- Washington

State rules vary widely.

**Estate Tax vs. Inheritance Tax: What's the Difference?**

- **Estate Tax:** Paid by the estate before money is distributed to heirs.
- **Inheritance Tax:** Paid by the heirs after receiving their inheritance.

**Action Step:**

Ask a CPA or estate attorney if your state has estate or inheritance taxes — especially if you live in the Northeast or Mid-Atlantic states.

**Real-World Example: Paul's Story**

Paul inherited $250,000 from his wife's IRA.

He lived in Pennsylvania, which has an inheritance tax — but because he was a spouse, his inheritance was **exempt**.

Many states **do not tax inheritances between spouses** — but check to be sure.

## Part 4: Deductions Widowers May Qualify For

You may qualify for certain tax deductions and credits after the death of a spouse.

### *1. Standard Deduction*

If you file as Married Filing Jointly (in the year of death) or as a Qualifying Widow(er) (the following two years), you qualify for:

- A higher standard deduction

- Lower tax brackets

## *2. Medical Expenses Deduction*

Grief often brings high medical costs —

final care for your spouse, funeral expenses, grief counseling, etc.

You can deduct unreimbursed medical expenses **above 7.5% of your adjusted gross income (AGI).**

**Examples of Deductible Expenses:**

- Hospice care
- Nursing home costs
- Medical equipment
- Doctor's bills
- Mental health therapy related to grief

## *3. Mortgage Interest Deduction*

If you still own your home and have a mortgage, you can deduct mortgage interest (subject to limits).

This can lower your taxable income significantly.

## *4. Charitable Giving*

Many widowers honor their spouse's memory through donations to causes they cared about.

Charitable contributions can be tax-deductible if you itemize deductions.

**Real-World Example: Sam's Story**

Sam lost his wife to cancer.

He donated $5,000 to a cancer research foundation in her name.

By itemizing his deductions, Sam reduced his taxable income and found emotional healing in giving back.

**Action Step:**

Track major medical expenses and charitable donations throughout the year — not just at tax time.

Good records = bigger deductions.

## Part 5: Finding a Grief-Aware CPA

You are not just looking for someone who can crunch numbers.

You are looking for someone who understands that grief changes everything —

including how you handle money.

### *What to Look For in a Grief-Aware CPA:*

- **Patience:** They explain things clearly, without rushing or overwhelming you.
- **Compassion:** They understand emotional fog and decision fatigue.
- **Experience:** They have worked with widowed clients before.
- **Fiduciary Commitment:** They put your best interests first.

**Questions to Ask When Interviewing CPAs:**

- Have you worked with widowed clients before?
- How do you handle complex emotional situations during tax prep?
- Will you walk me through available deductions and special filing statuses?
- Can you coordinate with my estate attorney or financial advisor if needed?

**Red Flags to Watch For:**

- They rush you or act impatient when you're confused.
- They seem unaware of special widower rules (like Qualifying Widow(er) status).

- They focus only on technical jargon instead of listening to your goals and fears.

**Real-World Example: Jack's Story**

Jack worked with a CPA who didn't understand grief.

The CPA rushed him, ignored his questions, and left him feeling more stressed.

The following year, Jack switched to a CPA who had lost her own husband years before.

She was patient, clear, and reassuring —

and helped Jack not just file taxes, but rebuild confidence.

You deserve that kind of support.

## Closing Reflection: Taxes Aren't Just About Numbers — They're About Protecting Your Healing

Filing taxes after losing your spouse isn't just paperwork.

It's part of rebuilding your life.

It's part of protecting your financial dignity.

It's part of respecting the love you shared and honoring the life you are still living.

You are not just paying taxes.

You are securing peace.

You are protecting your future.

You are giving yourself the breathing room you need to keep moving forward.

And you are doing it with wisdom, courage, and heart.

One form at a time.

One step at a time.

One brave decision at a time.

You are not alone.

And your best days — yes, your best financial days too — are still ahead.

# Part 4: Rethinking Your Retirement and Investment Plan

When your spouse dies, the future you planned together shifts forever.

And so must your financial roadmap.

Part 4 of this book is about helping you **reclaim your future** —
not by clinging to what might have been,
but by thoughtfully, bravely, and wisely building what can still be.
In this section, we'll walk you through:

- How to re-evaluate your retirement plans based on your new life stage and income.
- How widowhood may affect Social Security, pensions, and retirement account distributions.
- How to think differently about investment risk, returns, and income needs in light of your changed situation.
- When to consolidate, update, or adjust investment accounts (and when not to).
- How to shift your investment strategy from aggressive growth to strategic protection — without fear, without shame, and without panic.
- How to set new retirement goals that reflect *your* values, priorities, and dreams today — not the ones you shared with someone else in another life stage.

- What questions to ask a financial advisor now (and how to find one who truly understands widowed clients).
- How to balance living for today while planning wisely for tomorrow — so your later years are secure, flexible, and dignified.

Throughout Part 4, you'll be encouraged to approach your financial future not with dread, but with cautious hope —

to realize that **rethinking your retirement and investments isn't giving up** —

it's choosing to protect, honor, and nurture the life you still have left to live.

This section isn't just about money.

It's about **dignity.**

**Choice.**

**Peace of mind.**

You'll leave Part 4 with more clarity, more confidence, and a renewed sense of ownership over your financial destiny —

ready to move into the next chapter of life on your own terms.

# Chapter 11: Retirement Accounts After a Spouse's Death

## Introduction: You Are the Steward of a New Financial Future

When your spouse passes away, it's not just your day-to-day life that changes.

It's your long-term financial plan too.

The retirement dreams you once built together — the trips, the freedom, the security — may now feel distant or uncertain.

You might wonder:

- What happens to the 401(k) or IRA now?
- What am I supposed to do with pension benefits?
- How do I make the smartest decisions without messing it up?

If you are feeling overwhelmed, frozen, or afraid to make a mistake — breathe.

You don't have to do everything overnight.

You just have to walk through it, one wise step at a time.

This chapter will guide you through:

- How spousal rollovers for IRAs and 401(k)s work
- What inherited IRA rules mean for you

- How to handle pension decisions with confidence

By the end, you'll feel more clear, more empowered, and more at peace about your financial future — even if that future looks different than you once imagined.

Let's begin where you are.

## Part 1: Understanding Spousal Rollovers for IRAs and 401(k)s

If your spouse had a 401(k) or an IRA (Traditional or Roth), you have important choices to make.

One of the most powerful options available to you is called the **spousal rollover**.

### *What Is a Spousal Rollover?*

A spousal rollover allows you to move your late spouse's retirement account into your own name —

treating it as if it was yours all along.

This can apply to:

- Traditional IRAs
- Roth IRAs
- 401(k)s
- 403(b)s

### *Why a Spousal Rollover Matters:*

- You delay required minimum distributions (RMDs) until **you** reach age 73.
- You gain more flexibility for investment decisions.
- You avoid immediate taxation.
- You continue tax-deferred or tax-free growth (depending on account

type).

### *How a Spousal Rollover Works:*

**Step 1:**

Contact the financial institution managing your spouse's account.

**Step 2:**

Request a spousal rollover form or set up a meeting with an advisor.

**Step 3:**

Decide whether to roll the funds into your existing IRA (if you have one) or open a new IRA in your name.

**Step 4:**

Complete the paperwork carefully.

Avoid taking possession of the money yourself — this could trigger taxes.

**Pros of a Spousal Rollover:**

- Maintains tax advantages.
- Simplifies long-term planning.
- Allows you to name your own beneficiaries for the account.

**Cons of a Spousal Rollover:**

- If you're under age 59½ and need the money, early withdrawals could incur penalties.
- Once rolled over, the money is fully yours — subject to your own RMDs and rules.

**Real-World Example: Rick's Story**

Rick's wife passed away at 67.

She had a 401(k) with $250,000 saved.

Instead of cashing it out and paying taxes, Rick rolled the 401(k) into his own IRA.

Now, he controls the investments, delays RMDs until he needs them, and honors his wife's hard work by using the funds wisely for his future.

## Part 2: Inherited IRA Rules (Required Minimum Distributions)

If you don't do a full spousal rollover, or if you choose to set up an **inherited IRA**,

different rules apply — especially about **Required Minimum Distributions (RMDs).**

Let's walk through it calmly.

### *What Is an Inherited IRA?*

An inherited IRA is a special type of account that allows you to keep your late spouse's retirement money separate from your own accounts.

### *Why Choose an Inherited IRA?*

- You're under age 59½ and might need penalty-free access to the money.
- You don't want to delay RMDs until your retirement age.
- You want flexibility while you're still figuring out your financial future.

### *How RMDs Work for Inherited IRAs:*

If you inherit a Traditional IRA:

- You must start taking RMDs by **December 31st of the year after your spouse's death.**
- The amount you must withdraw depends on your life expectancy (the IRS provides tables).

If you inherit a Roth IRA:

- Generally, RMDs are not required for Roth IRAs that are properly rolled over into your own name.
- If you keep it as an inherited Roth IRA, RMDs may apply — but withdrawals remain tax-free.

**Pros of Keeping an Inherited IRA:**

- Access funds penalty-free even if under age 59½.
- Gradual distributions spread over many years.
- Some emotional comfort in maintaining the separation.

**Cons:**

- You must start taking RMDs sooner.
- More complicated paperwork and tracking.
- Less long-term tax advantage compared to a spousal rollover.

**Real-World Example: Susan's Story**

Susan was 58 when her husband died.

She chose to open an inherited IRA so she could access some of the funds penalty-free if needed,

rather than locking them away until age 59½.

Her choice gave her flexibility during a time of emotional and financial transition.

There is no one right answer.

Only the answer that best supports your healing and future security.

## Part 3: Pension Options — Survivor Benefits, Lump Sums, Ongoing Payments

If your spouse was receiving or was about to receive a pension, you may have critical decisions to make about survivor benefits.

Let's walk through it step-by-step.

### *Step 1: Understand What Was Chosen*

When your spouse retired (or was eligible to retire), they likely made an election about survivor benefits:

- **Single Life Annuity:**
- Payments stop at death.
- No continued payments to you.
- **Joint and Survivor Annuity:**
- A portion (often 50%–100%) of the pension continues to you for life.

**Find the paperwork.**

Understand what was selected.

### *Step 2: Your Choices If a Survivor Option Was Elected*

- **Continue Monthly Payments:**
- You continue receiving a portion of your spouse's pension each month.
- **Lump Sum Payout (if offered):**
- You may have the option to take a lump sum payout instead of ongoing payments.

**Pros of Monthly Payments:**

- Predictable income.
- Lifetime security.

**Cons of Monthly Payments:**

- May be reduced significantly compared to the original amount.
- No control over investment growth.

**Pros of a Lump Sum:**

- Immediate access to funds.
- Potential for growth if invested wisely.

**Cons of a Lump Sum:**

- Risk of poor investment returns.
- Temptation to spend too quickly.
- Loss of guaranteed lifetime income.

**Real-World Example: Bob's Story**

Bob's wife had a pension that offered him $1,200/month for life after her death.

At 68, Bob chose to continue receiving monthly payments rather than take a $180,000 lump sum.

The predictable income gave him peace of mind —
and let him focus on healing, not managing investments during grief.

**Action Step:**

Ask yourself:

- Do I need guaranteed monthly income to feel secure?
- Am I comfortable managing a large investment myself (or with an advisor)?
- What feels safer emotionally and financially for me right now?

There's no wrong answer —
only the answer that protects your peace.

## Part 4: Pros and Cons of Key Retirement Account Decisions for Widowers

**Spousal Rollover**

Pros:

- Full control of the account.
- Long-term tax advantages.
- Delays RMDs until your retirement age.

Cons:

- Early withdrawals (before 59½) may trigger penalties.

**Inherited IRA**

Pros:

- Penalty-free access to funds even before 59½.
- Gentle, gradual distributions.

Cons:

- Required Minimum Distributions start sooner.
- Slightly more complicated account management.

**Survivor Pension Payments**

Pros:

- Lifetime guaranteed income.
- Stability during emotional recovery.

Cons:

- Reduced payments compared to the original pension.
- Less flexibility.

**Lump Sum Pension Payout**

Pros:

- Full access to a large amount of cash.
- Opportunity to invest or use as needed.

Cons:

- Risk of poor investment choices.
- Loss of guaranteed income.

## Closing Reflection: Your Retirement Accounts Are Seeds — Not Shackles

The money your spouse worked so hard to save isn't just numbers on paper.

It's love.

It's sacrifice.

It's dreams —

dreams that can still nourish your future, even if they grow in different soil now.

You are not just managing money.

You are tending to your future.

Every choice you make — rollover, inherited IRA, pension decision —

is a way of honoring both the life you shared and the life you still deserve to live.

You don't have to figure it all out today.

You just have to keep choosing wisely, patiently, bravely.

And know this:

Your future is still rich with possibility.

Your financial stability is still within reach.

Your next chapter is still worth building —
and you are more than strong enough to build it.

# Chapter 12: Investing After Loss

## Introduction: Building a New Relationship with Risk, Growth, and Trust

After losing your spouse, everything feels more fragile.

More uncertain.

More vulnerable.

That includes your relationship with money — especially when it comes to investing.

Before, investing might have felt like a shared journey.

Now it might feel like an unfamiliar, even dangerous, territory — a place where one wrong step could undo everything you have left.

If you're feeling hesitant, scared, overwhelmed, or distrustful right now —

you are not alone.

This chapter is here to help you approach investing after loss with:

- Compassion for where you are emotionally
- Clarity about your real needs
- Practical, non-rushed steps toward rebuilding financial security

You don't have to figure everything out today.

You don't have to be perfect.

You just have to stay steady.

Let's begin where you are — not where you think you "should" be.

## Part 1: Should You Change Your Investment Strategy Now?

The first and most important rule after loss:

**Do not make big investment decisions right away — unless absolutely necessary.**

Grief clouds judgment.

It alters risk tolerance.

It amplifies fear and urgency.

Even the smartest, most experienced people make poor investment choices when grief is raw.

**Real-World Example: Bill's Story**

Bill inherited $500,000 from his wife's retirement accounts.

Within two months, feeling scared and pressured, he put it all into a risky real estate venture a friend recommended.

The venture collapsed.

Bill lost almost everything.

If Bill had paused —

taken a breath —

sought neutral advice —

he might have made very different decisions.

### *General Rule After Loss:*

- **First 6–12 Months:** Preserve what you have.
- Keep money safe in cash, CDs, conservative investments.
- Resist pressure to invest aggressively or take major risks.
- Focus on emotional healing, not financial performance.
- **After 12 Months:** Reevaluate your goals, risk tolerance, and long-term needs with a calmer heart and clearer mind.

*Exceptions to the Rule:*

- If you have immediate income needs and no other options, you may need to act sooner.
- If you are already very comfortable managing investments and feel confident, careful moves may be okay.

But for most widowers:

**Time is your ally.**

**Patience is your strategy.**

## Part 2: Understanding Risk Tolerance After a Major Life Change

Risk tolerance isn't just a number on a quiz.

It's a deeply emotional relationship with uncertainty, change, and loss.

And after losing your spouse, your risk tolerance often changes — sometimes dramatically.

*Signs Your Risk Tolerance May Have Shifted:*

- Feeling much more fearful about losing money.
- Valuing stability over growth.
- Preferring smaller, steady returns to big, volatile opportunities.
- Feeling emotionally upset after small market drops that wouldn't have bothered you before.

*That's Normal.*

You are not weak.

You are not bad at money.

You are human — and your whole emotional wiring has shifted.

### *How to Rethink Risk Tolerance:*

Step 1:

Acknowledge that it's okay for your investment style to change after loss.

Step 2:

Focus on what you need most right now:

- Security?
- Income?
- Flexibility?

Step 3:

Build an investment plan that feels emotionally sustainable — not just mathematically "optimal."

**Real-World Example: George's Story**

George was an aggressive investor before his wife died — heavily into stocks and real estate.

After her death, volatility made him sick with anxiety.

He moved 60% of his portfolio into bonds and cash equivalents.

He slept better.

He felt safer.

Was he giving up some growth?

Maybe.

But he was gaining something much more important:

**Peace of mind.**

And that matters more than beating an index.

## Part 3: Common Scams Targeting Widowers

Here's one of the cruelest truths:

Widowers are often targeted by scammers, con artists, and unethical "advisors" in the months and years after loss.

You are seen as vulnerable.

And some people — shamefully — prey on that.

*Common Scams:*

- **"Guaranteed" High-Return Investments:**
- Promises of 10%–20% returns with "no risk."
- Reality: If it sounds too good to be true, it is.
- **"Exclusive" Opportunities:**
- Pressure to "act fast" or "miss out."
- Reality: Real investments don't have ticking clocks.
- **"Free" Financial Seminars:**
- Heavy sales pitches disguised as education.
- Reality: Their goal is often to sell you expensive, unnecessary products.
- **Romance Scams:**
- Meeting someone online who quickly "needs" financial help.
- Reality: Emotional manipulation at its worst.
- **Unsolicited Calls/Emails from Fake Financial Companies:**
- Reality: Legitimate advisors do not cold-call widowers asking for money.

*Red Flags:*

- Urgency
- Secrecy
- Pressure
- Promises that seem "too good"
- Requests for personal financial information too early

**Real-World Example: Robert's Story**

Robert lost his wife and started getting calls about a "guaranteed 15% return investment in overseas real estate."

It sounded wonderful — until he noticed they kept dodging his questions about risks.

Robert trusted his instincts, hung up, and reported the scam.

### *Action Step:*

**Golden Rule:**

If you feel pressured, confused, or rushed — stop.

Good investments and good advisors respect your right to move slowly and understand fully.

Always.

## Part 4: Red Flags When Meeting Advisors

Not all financial advisors are created equal.

Some are:

- Highly ethical and skilled professionals who truly care.
- Others are glorified salespeople pushing products you don't need.

You need someone who will act as a **fiduciary** — legally required to put your best interests first.

### *Red Flags When Interviewing Advisors:*

- They talk more than they listen.
- They push products (annuities, life insurance, private investments) before understanding your goals.
- They dodge your questions about fees.
- They focus on investment returns instead of your broader financial needs.
- They make you feel rushed, stupid, or dependent.

**Good Advisors:**

- Listen deeply first.
- Educate without pressure.
- Disclose all fees openly.
- Treat you like an empowered partner, not a helpless victim.

**Real-World Example: Charles's Story**

Charles met with an advisor who spent the first meeting pitching expensive annuities.

Charles felt uncomfortable and left.

He later found a fee-only fiduciary advisor who helped him build a balanced plan, update his estate documents, and feel respected.

Trust your gut.

You deserve someone who treats your future — and your grief — with dignity.

## Closing Reflection: Investing After Loss Is About Protection, Not Perfection

You don't have to be the smartest investor in the room.

You don't have to beat the market.

You just have to:

- Protect your dignity.
- Protect your peace of mind.
- Protect your financial future.

Investing after loss isn't about chasing returns.

It's about honoring the life you still have left to live — wisely, patiently, steadily.

You are not fragile.

You are not helpless.

You are not a target.

You are a builder.

A protector.

A leader of your own next chapter.

And every wise, steady decision you make with your investments is a powerful act of survival, resilience, and hope.

Your best financial days are not behind you.

They are still ahead —

and you are walking toward them with strength.

One choice at a time.

One dollar at a time.

One hopeful step at a time.

# Chapter 13: Social Security Planning for Widowers

## Introduction: Social Security Isn't Just a Check — It's a Foundation

When you lose a spouse, your financial world shifts dramatically. And one of the biggest — and often most confusing — pieces of that shift is **Social Security**.

Questions come fast:

- Am I eligible for my spouse's benefits?
- Should I claim survivor benefits now, or wait?
- How does remarriage affect what I can collect?
- Should I switch from survivor benefits to my own work record later?

It's a lot to process — especially when you're already carrying so much emotionally.

But here's the good news:

**You don't have to know everything today.**

**You just have to understand your options.**

This chapter will guide you through:

- How survivor benefits work

- How they interact with your own work history
- How remarriage affects your rights
- Smart strategies for maximizing your Social Security income over your lifetime

We'll walk through it clearly, patiently, and without pressure.

Because Social Security isn't just about monthly checks.

It's about securing the dignity, stability, and freedom you deserve after profound loss.

## Part 1: Survivor Benefits — What They Are and How They Work

Let's start simple.

If your spouse worked and paid into Social Security,
you may be eligible for **survivor benefits** based on their work record.

### *Basic Facts About Survivor Benefits:*

- You can start collecting as early as **age 60** (or **50** if you are disabled).
- You must have been married to your spouse for at least **nine months** (with some exceptions for accidental deaths).
- You do not need to have worked yourself to qualify for survivor benefits.
- If you were divorced, you may still qualify if the marriage lasted **at least 10 years** and you haven't remarried before age 60.

### *How Much You Can Receive:*

Survivor benefits are based on your spouse's Social Security earnings.

Generally:

- You may receive **100%** of your deceased spouse's benefit if you claim at your full retirement age (FRA).

- If you claim before your FRA (say at 60), your survivor benefit will be **reduced**.

### *Full Retirement Age (FRA) for Survivor Benefits:*

Your FRA for survivor benefits is based on your year of birth:

- Born 1956 or earlier: FRA is 66
- Born 1962 or later: FRA is 67
- Born between 1957–1961: FRA gradually increases

**Real-World Example: John's Story**

John lost his wife at 62.

He was eligible to collect **reduced survivor benefits** immediately — or wait until his FRA and collect a **full survivor benefit**.

After consulting a financial advisor, John chose to delay until 66.

The higher monthly check gave him better long-term security.

**Action Step:**

Find out your spouse's Social Security benefit amount (contact the SSA or check their latest statement) and your own FRA for survivor benefits.

This information will guide smart decisions later.

## Part 2: Survivor Benefits vs. Your Own Work Record

One of the most confusing aspects of Social Security is how your **own benefits** and **survivor benefits** interact.

Let's clear it up carefully.

### *You Cannot Collect Both Full Benefits at the Same Time.*

You can:

- Collect one benefit first (either yours or survivor benefits)

- Later switch to the other if it pays more

### Scenario 1: Survivor Benefits First, Then Switch to Own Benefits

If your own Social Security retirement benefit will eventually be **higher** than your survivor benefit:

- You can start with survivor benefits at age 60 (or FRA if you want full benefit)
- Then switch to your own higher retirement benefit at age 70 (after it grows with delayed retirement credits)

### Scenario 2: Own Benefits First, Then Switch to Survivor Benefits

If your survivor benefit is **higher** than your own benefit:

- You could start your own retirement benefit early.
- Later switch to a higher survivor benefit at your FRA.

### Real-World Example: Michelle's Story

Michelle was 60 when her husband died.

Her own Social Security benefit at 62 would have been $1,200/month.

Her survivor benefit at 66 would be $2,100/month.

Michelle chose to collect a small early retirement benefit at 62 —
then switch to her full survivor benefit at 66.

This strategy helped bridge her income gap without locking in permanently lower survivor payments.

**Important Note:**

Once you start either benefit early, reductions and rules apply.

Strategic timing can significantly impact your lifetime income.

**Action Step:**

Create a simple chart comparing:

- Your estimated survivor benefits at different ages
- Your own Social Security benefits at different ages

Compare and see which path gives you the most lifetime income.

## Part 3: Remarrying and Its Impact on Survivor Benefits

Love may find you again.

If it does, your Social Security planning will need a fresh look.

### *How Remarriage Affects Survivor Benefits:*

- If you **remarry before age 60**, you generally lose the right to collect survivor benefits based on your deceased spouse.
- If you **remarry after age 60**, you **can still collect survivor benefits** based on your deceased spouse.

**Real-World Example: David's Story**

David was 59 when he fell in love again.

He and his partner decided to wait until David turned 60 to marry — ensuring he could still collect his late wife's survivor benefits.

That decision preserved nearly $300,000 in lifetime Social Security income.

**Special Notes for Divorced Widowers:**

- Same rules apply: remarriage before 60 generally disqualifies you from divorced survivor benefits.
- Remarriage after 60 does not.

**Action Step:**

If you are considering remarriage, meet with a financial advisor or Social Security expert to map out the impact on your benefits.

This isn't about choosing love or money.

It's about being wise, informed, and empowered in your choices.

## Part 4: Claiming Strategies for Maximizing Income

Here are common smart strategies widowers use:

### *Strategy 1: Delay Survivor Benefits if Possible*

If you can afford to wait until your FRA, your survivor benefit will be larger —

often 25%–30% higher than claiming early.

### *Strategy 2: Take Own Benefits Early, Switch Later*

Start your own Social Security benefit at age 62,
then switch to survivor benefits at your FRA if they are larger.

### *Strategy 3: Survivor Benefits First, Own Benefits Later*

Start survivor benefits early to bring in income.

Allow your own retirement benefit to grow with **delayed retirement credits** (about 8% per year) until age 70.

Switch to your higher personal benefit at 70.

**Real-World Example: Anne's Story**

Anne's husband passed away when she was 59.

She started her survivor benefits at 60 to cover basic expenses.

Meanwhile, her own Social Security retirement benefits kept growing.

At 70, she switched to her own benefit — now significantly larger — and secured a better retirement for her later years.

**Action Step:**

Use Social Security calculators (available on SSA.gov) or meet with a professional to model multiple claiming scenarios before deciding.

The wrong decision could cost you tens of thousands over your lifetime.

## Closing Reflection: Social Security Is More Than Money — It's Your Right to Dignity

You earned this.

Your spouse earned this.

Survivor benefits are not charity.

They are part of a promise you both contributed to —

a promise that your future would be protected even after profound loss.

Claiming wisely is not greed.

It is stewardship.

It is protecting your right to heal, to rebuild, to live with dignity and hope.

You are not alone.

You are not without choices.

You are not powerless.

You are the steady hand now —

for yourself, for your family, for the life you are still so worthy of living.

And every wise step you take with Social Security

is a step toward a future richer in security, dignity, and peace.

One decision at a time.

One courageous breath at a time.

You are doing better than you think.

And your next chapter is still filled with promise.

# Part 5: Long-Term Planning and Moving Forward

By the time you reach this section of the book, you've already walked through some of the hardest, most immediate financial decisions that follow loss.

You've stabilized.

You've organized.

You've begun to reclaim a sense of security.

Now, it's time to think longer-term.

**Part 5 is about building a future — not just surviving the present.**

This section gently guides you through:

- Rethinking what "retirement" means for you now — and how to create a new vision for your later years that fits your life today, not the life you once planned with someone else.
- How to revisit estate planning — updating wills, trusts, healthcare directives, and powers of attorney — to reflect your new reality and protect the people you love.
- How to care for adult children, aging parents, or others without sacrificing your own financial future — balancing generosity with wisdom.
- How to manage major life transitions — like downsizing, relocating, or even starting a new career or passion project in your later years.

- How to build a long-term financial plan that is flexible, resilient, and grounded in who you are now — not who you used to be.
- How to start dreaming again, without guilt or fear — and how to structure your finances to support those dreams.

Throughout Part 5, you'll be reminded that **your future is not canceled.**
It is still full of possibility, purpose, and meaning.
You'll leave this section not just with a financial checklist —
but with a deeper sense of confidence, dignity, and empowerment.
This isn't about "moving on."
It's about **moving forward** —
with wisdom, courage, and a future you design on your own terms.
You are not finished.
You are just getting started.

# Chapter 14: Healthcare and Insurance Updates

## Introduction: Your Health, Your Safety Net, Your Peace of Mind

When you lose your spouse, your world doesn't just change emotionally.

It also changes practically — and few areas become more vulnerable, or more urgent, than healthcare.

Questions come fast and heavy:

- Am I still covered under their health insurance?
- What happens to our Medicare plans?
- Do I need new coverage now?
- How do I plan for long-term care without them?

The truth is, health insurance isn't just paperwork after loss.

It's protection.

It's peace of mind.

It's a critical piece of rebuilding a life that is safe, stable, and secure.

This chapter will walk you through:

- What happens to health insurance after a spouse dies

- What to know about Medicare, COBRA, employer plans, and private insurance
- How to think about long-term care planning now
- How to make wise, steady healthcare decisions — without panic or pressure

You don't have to figure it all out today.

You just have to start understanding your options, and protecting your future, one wise step at a time.

Let's walk through it — together.

## Part 1: Health Insurance Changes After Losing a Spouse

When your spouse dies, your health insurance situation can change immediately — or slowly over several months, depending on how you were covered.

Understanding what coverage you have **right now** is the first priority.

### *Scenario 1: You Were Covered Under Your Spouse's Employer Plan*

- Most employer plans allow coverage to continue temporarily under **COBRA** (more on this soon).
- You typically have **60 days** to elect COBRA coverage.
- COBRA can last up to **36 months** in the case of widowhood.

### *Scenario 2: You Were Both on Medicare*

- If you were both enrolled in Medicare (Part A, B, C, D), your Medicare coverage remains **unchanged**.
- However, if you had a **Medicare Advantage Plan (Part C)** or a **Medicare Supplement (Medigap)** policy that was connected to your spouse's plan, you may need to update or re-enroll in a new policy.

### *Scenario 3: You Had Private Insurance*

- If you had a joint private plan, you'll need to contact the insurer to update the policy to reflect your new status.
- You may be eligible for a **Special Enrollment Period** to choose a new plan.

**Real-World Example: Tom's Story**

Tom, 64, was covered under his wife's employer health plan.
After she passed, he had 60 days to elect COBRA to continue coverage.
He chose COBRA to bridge the gap until he qualified for Medicare at 65.
Planning calmly gave him breathing room.

**Action Step:**

Contact your insurance provider or your late spouse's employer HR department immediately after loss to understand:

- When your current coverage ends
- What options you have for continuation
- What deadlines you must meet to avoid gaps

## Part 2: Understanding COBRA — Short-Term Bridge Coverage

**COBRA** stands for the **Consolidated Omnibus Budget Reconciliation Act** — a law that lets you temporarily continue your group health coverage after events like death, divorce, or job loss.

### *Key Facts About COBRA:*

- You must elect COBRA within **60 days** of losing coverage.
- You pay **100% of the premium** (plus a small administrative fee).
- Coverage can last up to **36 months** after the death of a spouse.
- COBRA covers the same doctors, networks, and services you had

before.

**Pros of Choosing COBRA:**

- No need to switch doctors or plans immediately.
- Provides stability during an emotional, chaotic time.

**Cons of Choosing COBRA:**

- Expensive — you pay the full premium, not just the employee portion.
- It's temporary — you'll still need a long-term solution.

**Real-World Example: Frank's Story**

Frank's wife had excellent employer coverage.

After she passed, he chose COBRA to continue coverage for 18 months — then transitioned to Medicare when he turned 65.

That strategy minimized disruption and protected his health during a vulnerable time.

**Action Step:**

Even if COBRA is expensive, consider using it **short-term** to avoid uninsured periods while you explore permanent options.

## Part 3: Medicare Considerations for Widowers

If you're over 65 (or approaching it), **Medicare** becomes your primary insurance safety net.

Losing a spouse may trigger opportunities — and requirements — to update your coverage.

### *Medicare Basics:*

- **Part A:** Hospital insurance (usually free if you or your spouse paid Medicare taxes)
- **Part B:** Medical insurance (monthly premium required)
- **Part C:** Medicare Advantage plans (private insurance alternatives to Original Medicare)
- **Part D:** Prescription drug plans

### *What You Need to Do After Spouse's Death:*

- Notify Medicare about the death.
- Update billing if premiums were paid jointly.
- Review your Medicare Advantage or Supplement Plan:
- Some plans allow surviving spouses to stay enrolled.
- Others require you to enroll in a new plan.

**Special Enrollment Period (SEP):**

Widowers may qualify for a Special Enrollment Period to:

- Join a new Medicare Advantage or Part D plan.
- Switch back to Original Medicare if preferred.

**Real-World Example: Betty's Story**

Betty, 67, was on a joint Medicare Advantage plan with her husband.

After his death, she was eligible to either continue with the insurer under a new individual plan or switch to a new plan entirely without penalty.

She chose a new plan that better fit her single lifestyle and medical needs.

**Action Step:**

Schedule a Medicare review immediately after loss to ensure you're properly covered and not overpaying for services you no longer need.

## Part 4: Long-Term Care Considerations for Widowers

Planning for long-term care after loss can feel overwhelming — but it's critical to protecting your independence and your financial dignity.

### *What Is Long-Term Care?*

- Help with daily activities like bathing, dressing, eating, and mobility.
- Provided in-home, in assisted living, or in nursing facilities.

### *Why Long-Term Care Planning Matters Even More Now:*

- You no longer have a spouse to be your default caregiver.
- Paying for care out-of-pocket can quickly deplete savings.
- Long-term care costs are rising each year.

### *Options for Covering Long-Term Care:*

- **Self-Insurance:** Saving enough to cover future costs.
- **Long-Term Care Insurance:** Standalone policies or riders attached to life insurance.
- **Hybrid Policies:** Combine life insurance and long-term care coverage.
- **Government Programs:** Medicaid (only for low-income individuals).

**Pros and Cons of Long-Term Care Insurance:**

**Pros:**

- Protects savings.
- Provides peace of mind.
- Broad coverage options.

**Cons:**

- Can be expensive.
- Premiums can increase.
- May be difficult to qualify for after a certain age or health condition.

**Real-World Example: Richard's Story**

Richard, 68, lost his wife and realized he no longer had an at-home caregiver if he became disabled.

He purchased a hybrid life/long-term care insurance policy — protecting his assets while securing care options if needed.

It wasn't cheap, but it gave him emotional security and dignity.

**Action Step:**

Talk to a licensed, fiduciary financial planner or insurance specialist about whether long-term care coverage fits your situation.

Don't put this off.

Options narrow with age and health changes.

## Part 5: Updating or Reevaluating Health Insurance

After losing a spouse, it's crucial to **review all your health-related policies**:

- Health insurance
- Medicare Advantage or Supplement plans
- Long-term care insurance
- Life insurance with health riders
- Disability insurance (if still working)

### *Why Updates Matter:*

- Your needs may have changed dramatically.
- Premiums may no longer be optimized for your solo lifestyle.
- Coverage gaps could leave you vulnerable in a medical emergency.

**Checklist for Reevaluating Health Insurance After Loss:**

- Confirm your current health insurance coverage status.
- Identify if COBRA, private, or Medicare coverage is your best bridge.
- Update beneficiaries on any insurance policies.
- Compare Medicare Advantage and Supplement options annually.
- Consider new or updated long-term care solutions.
- Meet with a fiduciary advisor or Medicare specialist for unbiased guidance.

## Closing Reflection: Your Health Is Your First Wealth

Without health, freedom becomes harder to hold onto.
Without smart insurance decisions, financial freedom becomes fragile.
Your health, your security, your dignity —
they are worth protecting fiercely and wisely.
You are not just navigating healthcare and insurance.
You are building a shield around your future.
You are standing guard over the life you still have left to live.
You don't have to be an expert.
You don't have to know everything at once.
You just have to be steady.
Patient.
Wise.
And you already are.
Every form you complete.
Every policy you review.
Every appointment you make.
They are acts of hope.
Acts of protection.
Acts of profound strength.
Your life is still worthy of fierce care.
And you are doing better than you know.

# Chapter 15: Housing and Real Estate Decisions

## Introduction: Home Is Where the Heart Is — And Where the Hard Choices Begin

When you lose your spouse, your house doesn't just feel emptier.

It feels different.

Sometimes it feels too big.

Sometimes too lonely.

Sometimes like the only thing still tying you to a life you desperately miss.

Deciding what to do about your home is one of the most emotional — and financial — crossroads widowers face.

Should you stay?

Sell?

Rent it out?

Downsize?

Relocate?

There's no one right answer.

Only the answer that's right for you — right for your heart, and right for your finances.

This chapter will walk you through:

- How to think about keeping, selling, or renting your home
- How to balance emotional and financial factors wisely
- How to evaluate mortgage, property taxes, and maintenance realistically
- How to approach downsizing without guilt or fear

You don't have to rush this decision.

You don't have to get it perfect.

You just have to move forward thoughtfully.

Let's begin.

## Part 1: Should You Keep, Sell, or Rent Your Home?

Your home holds memories.

But it also holds expenses, responsibilities, and possibilities.

Choosing what to do with it is one of the biggest decisions you'll face after loss.

Let's walk through your options carefully.

### *Option 1: Keeping the Home*

Many widowers initially choose to stay:

- The home feels safe, familiar, comforting.
- Moving feels like losing one more thing.
- They want stability for themselves or their children.

**Pros:**

- Emotional comfort during grief.
- No immediate disruption.
- Keeps community ties, neighbors, and routines.

**Cons:**

- Mortgage payments may now be too heavy for one income.
- Property taxes, utilities, insurance, and maintenance add up.
- The home may no longer fit your future lifestyle or needs.

### *Option 2: Selling the Home*

Some widowers decide to sell:

- The house feels too big, empty, or painful.
- Financially, it makes sense to free up equity.
- They want a fresh start in a new place.

**Pros:**

- Frees up capital to invest, save, or downsize.
- Reduces ongoing financial and physical burdens.
- Symbolically starts a new chapter.

**Cons:**

- Emotional pain of leaving memories behind.
- Moving can be physically and mentally overwhelming.
- Housing markets may be volatile.

### *Option 3: Renting the Home*

Some widowers turn their home into a rental:

- They're not ready to sell emotionally.
- They want ongoing rental income.
- They move elsewhere but keep the home for now.

**Pros:**

- Provides passive income.
- Home can appreciate while being rented.
- Keeps the door open for returning later.

**Cons:**

- Managing tenants can be stressful.
- Property management fees eat into profits.
- Emotional ties can make being a landlord difficult.

**Real-World Example: Paul's Story**

Paul, 67, stayed in the family home for three years after his wife died.

Eventually, the maintenance overwhelmed him.

He sold the house, bought a smaller condo closer to his grandchildren, and never looked back.

Paul says it took him time to be ready — and that's okay.

There's no timeline.

Only your timeline.

**Action Step:**

Write down your emotional reasons and financial reasons for keeping, selling, or renting your home.

Seeing them side-by-side can bring surprising clarity.

## Part 2: Emotional vs Financial Factors — Balancing Heart and Head

You are not just making a financial decision.

You are making a deeply human one.

And it's okay — even healthy — to acknowledge that.

### *Emotional Reasons to Stay:*

- Connection to memories, shared life.
- Comfort of the familiar.
- Desire to avoid major change during grief.

### *Emotional Reasons to Leave:*

- Painful daily reminders.
- Too much house for one person.
- Desire for a fresh start, simpler living.

### *Financial Reasons to Stay:*

- Paid-off mortgage, low living costs.
- Affordable property taxes.
- Strategic location near support networks.

### *Financial Reasons to Leave:*

- High mortgage or maintenance costs.
- Opportunity to free up equity for retirement.
- Downsizing to lower living expenses.

### *Balancing Heart and Head:*

You don't have to choose cold logic over tender emotion.

You can honor both.

The goal is not to erase emotion — it's to **respect emotion while making sustainable choices.**

If staying gives you peace and is financially manageable, stay.

If leaving opens a path to healing and security, leave.

Both choices are brave.

**Real-World Example: Margaret's Story**

Margaret stayed in her big suburban home for two years after losing her husband.

At first, the idea of leaving made her physically ill.

Later, she realized her grief had softened — and her needs had changed.

She sold the home, moved to a smaller townhouse, and found new community and joy.

Give yourself permission to change your mind over time.

**Action Step:**

Ask yourself:

"Am I making this housing decision from fear? From love? From hope? From exhaustion?"

Name the emotions driving your thoughts — then layer financial facts on top.

You are allowed to bring your whole self to this decision.

## Part 3: How to Evaluate Mortgage, Property Taxes, and Maintenance Costs

Beyond emotions, hard numbers matter.

Let's walk through a clear, steady evaluation process.

### *Mortgage:*

- **Do you still owe on the mortgage?**
- **What is the monthly payment?**
- **Is it affordable on your new income?**

### *Property Taxes:*

- Property taxes can rise sharply depending on state laws after one spouse dies.
- Confirm with your local assessor's office if any exemptions or freezes

apply.

*Maintenance and Utilities:*

- Routine home repairs
- Landscaping
- HVAC servicing
- Roof repairs
- Water bills, electric bills, internet, security systems

Estimate annual maintenance costs at **1%–4% of your home's value**.

Example:

If your home is worth $300,000, budget $3,000–$12,000 per year for upkeep.

*Home Insurance:*

- Premiums may increase without bundling discounts.
- You may need to adjust coverage if ownership changes.

**Real-World Example: Daniel's Story**

Daniel realized that between property taxes, homeowners insurance, and maintenance, his beautiful 5-bedroom house was costing him over $2,500/month — before even counting utilities.

Downsizing freed up cash and reduced his stress overnight.

**Action Step:**

Create a simple monthly and yearly estimate of what your home truly costs now —

then decide if those numbers feel sustainable long-term.

## Part 4: Downsizing Tips for Widowers

If you decide to move, downsizing can feel overwhelming — emotionally and logistically.
Here's how to approach it steadily.

### *Tip 1: Start with One Small Area*

Don't tackle the whole house at once.

- Start with a closet.
- A single room.
- A single drawer.

Momentum builds confidence.

### *Tip 2: Keep Only What Supports Your Future Life*

Honor memories — but remember that **your future deserves space too.**
Keep what serves the life you are building now, not just the life you lost.

### *Tip 3: Get Help — Emotional and Physical*

You don't have to sort through a lifetime of belongings alone.

- Trusted family or friends
- Professional organizers
- Moving specialists

Asking for help is strength, not weakness.

### *Tip 4: Be Gentle with Yourself*

You are not "clearing out clutter."

You are **honoring a sacred transition.**

Move at your own pace.

Grieve, remember, release — at your own pace.

**Real-World Example: Jim's Story**

Jim, 70, decided to downsize after five years of living alone in his family home.

He kept meaningful keepsakes, gave treasured items to family, and sold or donated the rest.

Today, his cozy condo feels not like a loss — but like a renewal.

**Action Step:**

Create a downsizing plan:

- Which areas to tackle first
- What help you'll accept
- A simple 90-day timeline (not rushed)

## Closing Reflection: Your Home Is Where Your Next Chapter Begins

Your house was part of your past.

But it doesn't have to define your future.

Whether you stay, sell, rent, or relocate —

you are not losing love by moving forward.

You are carrying it with you.

You are honoring your memories

while making room for new memories still to come.

And you are strong enough, wise enough, and brave enough to choose what feels right for you —

emotionally, financially, and practically.

There is no shame in staying.

There is no shame in leaving.

There is only strength in building a future that fits the life you have now

—

and the life you deserve to keep living.

One room at a time.

One step at a time.

One courageous breath at a time.

# Chapter 16: Planning for Your Legacy

## Introduction: Building Something That Lasts Beyond You

After the loss of your spouse, it's easy to focus only on today: surviving, adjusting, making it through.

But at some point — quietly, patiently — a new question arises:

**What will I leave behind?**

Not just money.

Not just possessions.

But values.

Lessons.

Security.

Dignity.

This chapter isn't about preparing for death.

It's about **living wisely** — so that when your time comes, you've built a legacy that honors both you and the life you shared with the one you lost.

We'll walk through:

- Revisiting and updating your estate plans
- Protecting your heirs thoughtfully
- Having honest, loving conversations with adult children
- Giving back to causes close to your heart

You don't have to plan everything overnight.

But taking these steps, steadily, will give you peace of mind —
and give the people you love a precious gift: clarity, security, and the continuation of your love.

Let's begin.

## Part 1: Revisiting Wills, Trusts, and Powers of Attorney

When your spouse dies, your old estate plan — if you had one — is almost certainly out of date.

Updating it is not just paperwork.

It's an act of love.

### *Step 1: Update Your Will*

Your will likely named your spouse as a:

- Primary beneficiary
- Executor (the person responsible for carrying out your wishes)
- Guardian for minor children (if applicable)

Now, you need to:

- Choose new beneficiaries.
- Name a new executor.
- Update guardianship arrangements if needed.

**Real-World Example: Jim's Story**

Jim's original will left everything to his wife.

After her death, if he hadn't updated it, his estate could have gone through unnecessary probate delays — causing stress for his adult children.

He met with an estate attorney, updated his will, and made sure everything was clear, current, and enforceable.

**Action Step:**

Meet with an estate attorney (not just a general lawyer) to update your will within 6–12 months after loss.

### *Step 2: Review and Update Trusts*

If you and your spouse had a trust:

- Revocable living trusts
- Family trusts
- Charitable trusts

You'll need to:

- Retitle assets if necessary.
- Remove your spouse's name where appropriate.
- Appoint new successor trustees.

### *Step 3: Reassign Powers of Attorney*

Powers of attorney (for financial and medical decisions) often name your spouse as the primary agent.

You'll need to:

- Choose new agents (children, siblings, trusted friends).
- Make sure updated documents are signed, notarized, and shared with relevant parties.

**Why This Matters:**

Without updated powers of attorney, no one may be legally allowed to act for you if you become incapacitated —

forcing your loved ones into lengthy court processes.

**Action Step:**

Make updating your will, trusts, and powers of attorney a top priority —

ideally within your first or second year after your spouse's death.

## Part 2: How to Protect Your Heirs

Your children, grandchildren, or other heirs may be financially savvy — or they may be completely unprepared.

Protecting them doesn't mean controlling them.

It means setting up systems that support their stability, not stress.

### *Smart Ways to Protect Heirs:*

- **Clear Beneficiary Designations:**
- Update retirement accounts, life insurance, and bank accounts.
- **Trusts for Young or Vulnerable Beneficiaries:**
- Prevents lump sum inheritance mistakes.
- **Instructions for Digital Assets:**
- Email accounts, online banking, social media profiles.
- **Simple, Updated Legal Documents:**
- The easier you make it, the less conflict or confusion later.

**Real-World Example: Alan's Story**

Alan created a simple trust to distribute his estate equally among his three kids — but with staggered payments at ages 25, 30, and 35.

It protected them from blowing their inheritance at 22 — and preserved family harmony.

**Action Step:**

List all your assets and accounts.

Make sure every one of them has an updated, clear, coordinated beneficiary designation.

## Part 3: Talking to Adult Children About Your Wishes

One of the greatest gifts you can give your adult children is clarity.

Talking about your financial wishes, your health care preferences, and your legacy plans **before** something happens spares them enormous confusion and guilt later.

### *Why These Conversations Matter:*

- Reduces conflict between siblings or heirs.
- Prevents painful guessing games.
- Gives your family a roadmap to honor you with dignity.

### *How to Approach the Conversation:*

- Choose a calm, non-rushed setting.
- Frame it as an act of love, not fear.
- Be honest about your hopes, fears, and plans.
- Encourage their questions.

**Key Topics to Cover:**

- Who your financial and healthcare decision-makers are
- Where important documents are located
- What kind of end-of-life care you want
- How you want your estate handled
- Charitable giving or legacy goals

**Real-World Example: Laura's Story**

Laura gathered her three children for a quiet Sunday dinner.

She shared copies of her will, powers of attorney, and a letter explaining her funeral wishes.

Her children were emotional — but also deeply grateful.

When Laura later passed away peacefully, there were no arguments, no second-guessing, and no chaos.

Only love.

**Action Step:**

Schedule a "family legacy conversation" within the next six months.

Use it to open communication, not close it down.

## Part 4: Charitable Giving and Honoring Shared Causes

If you and your spouse shared a passion for certain causes, continuing that legacy can be a healing and powerful part of your estate plan.

### *Options for Charitable Giving:*

- **Gifts through your will or trust:**
- A simple bequest to a nonprofit.
- **Charitable remainder trusts:**
- Provides income to heirs now, and gifts to charity later.
- **Donor-advised funds:**
- Flexible way to set aside money for charitable giving with tax advantages.
- **Naming charities as beneficiaries:**
- On retirement accounts, life insurance, etc.

**Pros of Including Charitable Giving:**

- Honors shared values.
- Supports causes you believe in.
- Can reduce estate taxes if applicable.

**Real-World Example: Greg's Story**

Greg and his wife were passionate about animal rescue.

In his updated will, Greg designated 10% of his estate to their favorite animal shelter.

That gift not only honored their shared passion — it helped Greg feel that part of their love lived on in the world.

**Action Step:**

If charitable giving matters to you, add it to your estate plan — even a small amount makes a difference.

## Closing Reflection: Your Legacy Is a Love Letter to the Future

You're not just updating paperwork.

You are writing a love letter:

- To your children.
- To your grandchildren.
- To your community.
- To the world you leave behind.

You are not just leaving behind money.

You are leaving behind clarity, dignity, and stability.

You are making it easier for the people you love to grieve without confusion.

You are protecting them from unnecessary pain.

You are giving them the freedom to remember you with love, not legal battles.

And you are ensuring that the values you and your spouse cherished —
the life you built together —
continue to ripple outward long after you are gone.

You are not powerless.

You are a builder of futures.

One conversation at a time.

One signature at a time.

One brave step at a time.

Your best legacy won't just be measured in dollars.

It will be measured in peace, kindness, and love.

# Chapter 17: Giving Yourself Permission to Dream Again

## Introduction: Life After Loss Isn't Just Survival — It's Renewal

In the weeks and months after losing your spouse, just getting through the day can feel like a victory.

Dreaming again?

Setting new goals?

Finding joy?

That can feel impossible.

Or disloyal.

Or selfish.

But here's the truth:

**Healing doesn't mean forgetting.**

**Building a future doesn't mean betraying the past.**

**Living fully doesn't mean loving less.**

You are allowed —

not just allowed, but called —

to build a life worth living again.

This chapter will guide you through:

- How to set new financial goals that reflect who you are now
- How to weave joy, travel, hobbies, and experiences into your financial

life without guilt
- How to honor your spouse through thoughtful financial legacies — scholarships, family gifts, memorials

You are not starting over from scratch.

You are starting from strength.

Let's walk through it — one steady, hopeful step at a time.

## Part 1: Setting New Financial Goals — Without Guilt

When you planned your future with your spouse, every goal was a shared one.

Retirement plans.

Dream vacations.

Charities to support.

The home you would grow old in.

Now, it's different.

But different doesn't mean lesser.

It just means it's time to think differently about what you want, what you need, and what you are still called to create.

### *Why Financial Goals Still Matter:*

- They give direction to your money — and your energy.
- They create purpose beyond survival.
- They help you rebuild confidence after loss.

### *How to Set New Financial Goals:*

**Step 1: Grieve First, Plan Later**

Give yourself time.

Your first financial goal may simply be "stabilize emotionally and financially."

That's okay.

**Step 2: Reconnect to What Matters to You Now**

Ask yourself:

- What experiences do I still want to have?
- Who do I want to help?
- What legacy do I want to leave behind?

**Step 3: Prioritize Flexibility**

You are in a season of reinvention.

Goals should be **flexible**, not rigid.

It's okay if what you want today changes in five years.

**Step 4: Start Small**

Maybe you save for a trip.

Maybe you budget for a home improvement.

Maybe you set a giving goal.

Small steps create momentum.

**Real-World Example: Jerry's Story**

Jerry, 63, initially felt paralyzed after his wife's death.

After a year, he set a simple goal:

save $5,000 to take his grandchildren to Disneyland.

That goal became a light in the dark — something to look forward to, something to build toward.

**Action Step:**

Write down one new financial goal that feels exciting — or even just meaningful — to you right now.

Big or small, it matters.

## Part 2: Travel, Hobbies, and Experiences — Budgeting Joy into Your Life

You have a right to joy.

You have a right to wonder, to exploration, to beauty.

You have a right to **budget for it** — not as an indulgence, but as a necessity of healing.

### *Why Budgeting for Joy Matters:*

- Life isn't meant to be only about bills and survival.
- Experiences create meaning, not just material wealth.
- Joy strengthens resilience and mental health.

### *How to Budget Joyfully and Wisely:*

**Step 1: Name Your Dreams Without Self-Judgment**

What stirs your heart?

- Traveling?
- Painting?
- Restoring an old car?
- Visiting grandchildren?

Write it down — even if it feels frivolous.

**Step 2: Set a Joy Budget**

- 5%–10% of your annual spending could go toward joyful experiences.
- It can be structured (specific savings account) or informal (part of monthly cash flow).

**Step 3: Plan, Save, Anticipate**

- Put your trip or hobby in the calendar.
- Start a dedicated savings plan.
- Watch it grow — anticipation is half the joy.

**Step 4: Allow Yourself to Enjoy It Fully**

Guilt is not required.

Joy is not selfish.

Experiencing life honors the life you built — and the life you still have.

**Real-World Example: Sam's Story**

Sam, 70, decided to finally take the Alaskan cruise he and his wife had always dreamed about.

He went with friends.

He cried.

He laughed.

He lived.

And he came home renewed.

**Action Step:**

Create a "joy list" — 5 experiences or hobbies you would love to pursue.

Next to each, estimate a cost and start planning.

## Part 3: Honoring Your Spouse Financially

One powerful way to bridge past and future is to honor your spouse's memory with meaningful financial acts.

### *Options for Financial Honor:*

- **Scholarship Funds:**
- Set up a scholarship in their name at a school, university, or nonprofit.
- **Family Gifts:**
- Contribute toward a grandchild's education fund in your spouse's honor.
- **Charitable Memorials:**

- Donate annually to causes you supported together.
- **Memorial Projects:**
- Sponsor a park bench, library fund, or art installation in their memory.

**Pros of Honoring Financially:**

- Creates lasting good in their name.
- Provides you and your family a way to connect positively to grief.
- Builds a legacy of generosity.

**Real-World Example: Kevin's Story**

Kevin set up a $25,000 scholarship at his wife's alma mater, awarded each year to a nursing student.

Every spring, he attends the scholarship luncheon.

Seeing young students thrive because of his wife's legacy heals him in ways words can't explain.

**Action Step:**

If honoring your spouse financially resonates with you, start small:

Research causes or schools that mattered to them.

Schedule a call or meeting to explore options.

You don't have to be a millionaire to leave a legacy.

## Closing Reflection: You Are Allowed to Dream — Again and Again

You have permission to:

- Want more.
- Hope again.
- Build again.
- Laugh again.
- Love again.

Your spouse's death closed a chapter.

But it did not close the book.

There are still chapters to be written:

- Joyful ones.
- Adventurous ones.
- Meaningful ones.
- Hopeful ones.

You are still here.

You are still worthy.

You are still powerful.

And every dream you nurture now is not a betrayal of your past —

it is an act of gratitude for the life you shared, and for the life you still carry forward.

Your dreams honor your love story.

Your dreams honor your survival.

Your dreams honor the sacred, unbreakable truth:

That love does not end.

That hope does not die.

That life, even shattered, can be rebuilt — brilliantly, beautifully, bravely.

One dream at a time.

One joyful step at a time.

One courageous breath at a time.

# Part 6: Special Situations

Every widower's financial journey is unique.

While many of the steps you've learned so far — stabilizing, organizing, rebuilding — apply broadly, there are also moments when your path may take a turn that needs extra care, specialized knowledge, or simply more patience and understanding.

**Part 6: Special Situations** is here to meet you in those moments.

In this section, we'll explore some of the most common (and often most overwhelming) special situations widowers face, including:

- **Navigating Inheritance:** Receiving assets after your spouse's death — and how to handle them wisely without rushing or risking mistakes.
- **Blended Families and Second Marriages:** Updating your financial plans thoughtfully when new relationships and stepfamily dynamics come into the picture.
- **Widowed While Still Working:** How to balance grieving, career decisions, retirement contributions, and future planning while still in the workforce.
- **Sudden Wealth After Loss:** What to do if you suddenly inherit life insurance payouts, retirement accounts, or other significant assets — and how to protect, not squander, that wealth.
- **Widowers Facing Health Challenges:** Planning ahead for your own long-term care, medical needs, and financial dignity if your health situation changes.

Each chapter gently walks you through:

- The unique financial and emotional challenges that come with each situation.
- Step-by-step guidance on how to approach decisions calmly, wisely, and sustainably.
- Real-world examples of widowers who navigated these crossroads — and what they learned along the way.

You'll also find practical action steps, breakdowns of complex ideas in plain language, and grounded encouragement.

Because in special situations, it's even more important to slow down, breathe, and remember:

**You are not alone.**

**You are not behind.**

**You are not broken.**

You are simply facing another chapter of growth, courage, and healing — and you have everything it takes to walk it with strength.

# Chapter 18: Widowers with Minor Children

## Introduction: Carrying Their Grief, Carrying Their Future

Losing a spouse is devastating.

Losing a spouse **while raising minor children** adds an entire new dimension of heartbreak, pressure, and fear.

You are not just grieving your partner.

You are holding space for your children's grief too.

You are not just rebuilding your financial life.

You are shaping their financial future as well.

It's heavy.

It's exhausting.

It's overwhelming.

But it is also sacred work.

This chapter will walk with you — slowly, steadily — through:

- How to protect your children legally and financially
- How to manage money while raising grieving kids
- How to use life insurance wisely for their future
- How to start teaching basic financial skills even now

You don't have to be perfect.

You just have to stay present, steady, and willing.

And you already are.

Let's begin.

## Part 1: Guardianship and Trust Issues — Protecting Their Future If Something Happens to You

One of the most important — and emotionally difficult — tasks you face now is **restructuring your guardianship and trust plans**.

If you were to pass away unexpectedly, what happens to your children?

Who cares for them?

Who manages any assets for them?

How is their financial security protected?

This isn't just about paperwork.

It's about peace of mind — for you, and for them.

### *Step 1: Appoint a Legal Guardian*

A guardian is the person who will raise your children if you are no longer able to.

Without naming one in your will:

- The court decides.
- Family disputes can erupt.
- Your children's care could be delayed or disrupted.

**Choosing a Guardian: What to Consider:**

- Their ability and willingness to raise children
- Shared values and parenting styles
- Financial stability (although assets can be separated from custody)
- Relationship with your children
- Age and health

**Real-World Example: Mark's Story**

Mark named his sister and her husband as guardians for his two young daughters.

They lived nearby, shared similar values, and loved the girls deeply.

Mark said the process brought him peace — and strengthened family bonds.

## *Step 2: Set Up or Update a Trust*

Leaving assets directly to minors creates problems:

- Courts must appoint a custodian.
- Children may receive full access at 18 — often too young for wise decisions.
- Funds may be mismanaged.

Instead, consider a **trust**:

- A trustee manages funds according to your instructions.
- Distributions can be structured (e.g., partial access at ages 25, 30).
- The trustee can also pay for education, health, housing needs before the child reaches full adulthood.

**Action Step:**

Meet with an estate planning attorney to create or update your will, guardianship designations, and any necessary trusts for your minor children.

Do it within the next 6 months — no matter how uncomfortable it feels.

This is an act of profound love.

## Part 2: Managing Finances While Raising Grieving Kids

Raising children after losing your spouse adds emotional, physical, and financial demands.

And none of it comes with a handbook.

Here's how to approach it as steadily as possible.

### *Step 1: Redo Your Budget*

Your household budget must reflect:

- Loss of one income (if applicable)
- Changes in childcare needs
- Education expenses
- Therapy or counseling costs
- Emergency fund contributions

Expect fluctuations — and plan for flexibility.

### *Step 2: Prioritize Financial Stability*

Children need emotional security first —

but financial security is close behind.

Your focus should be:

- Keeping housing stable if possible
- Maintaining consistent routines
- Avoiding high-risk financial moves (e.g., quitting work, drastic investments)

### *Step 3: Tap Into Available Resources*

You may be eligible for:

- Social Security survivor benefits for minor children
- Scholarships and grants for kids who have lost a parent
- Community support programs (therapy subsidies, youth activities)

**Real-World Example: Robert's Story**

Robert lost his wife suddenly, leaving him to raise two middle-schoolers. He worked with a financial planner to:

- Structure a lean, sustainable budget
- Maximize survivor benefits
- Create college savings plans even on one income

It wasn't easy — but it gave his children the foundation they needed to feel safe again.

**Action Step:**

Create a new monthly budget centered on **stability first** — and adjust it quarterly as new needs or changes arise.

## Part 3: Life Insurance Considerations for Children

Life insurance becomes even more critical when you are the sole financial provider and protector.

### *Why Life Insurance Matters for Widowers with Kids:*

- Pays for immediate needs if you pass away unexpectedly
- Covers education, housing, healthcare
- Prevents financial hardship for guardians or surviving children

## *Key Decisions to Make:*

### How Much Coverage?

- A rough starting point: 7–10 times your annual income.
- Add additional coverage to pay off mortgage or fund college if desired.

### What Type of Policy?

- **Term Life Insurance:**
- Most affordable; coverage for a specific number of years.
- **Permanent Life Insurance (Whole or Universal):**
- More expensive; builds cash value; can last lifetime if maintained.

For most widowers, **term insurance** offers the best value during child-raising years.

### Who Should Be the Beneficiary?

- Not minor children directly (they cannot legally inherit).
- Instead, designate the trust you set up (see Part 1).
- Trustee will manage payouts according to your wishes.

### Real-World Example: Dave's Story

Dave increased his term life coverage to $750,000 after his wife's death —

enough to support his three kids through college if needed.

He set the trust as the beneficiary, ensuring the funds would be properly managed.

**Action Step:**

Review your current life insurance coverage.

If gaps exist, meet with a licensed, fiduciary advisor to secure appropriate policies within 90 days.

## Part 4: Teaching Kids Basic Financial Skills — Even in Grief

Teaching your children about money after loss is about more than dollars.

It's about building resilience.

It's about showing them that they have agency, stability, and hope — even after devastating change.

### *Age-Appropriate Financial Lessons:*

**Ages 5–10:**

- Understanding needs vs wants
- Saving a portion of any money they receive
- Simple conversations about generosity

**Ages 11–15:**

- Budgeting small allowances
- Setting savings goals for desired purchases
- Introduction to banking basics (opening a savings account)

**Ages 16–18:**

- Managing part-time job income
- Understanding credit basics
- Preparing for college costs and budgeting

### *Tips for Teaching Financial Resilience:*

- Be honest, but age-appropriate, about family financial realities.
- Involve them in small financial decisions (e.g., grocery budgeting, planning a family trip).
- Praise effort and planning, not just outcomes.

- Model healthy financial behavior yourself — budgeting, saving, giving.

**Real-World Example: Lisa's Story**

Lisa started involving her teenage sons in budgeting conversations after her husband died.

Together, they planned family vacations, prioritized spending, and celebrated savings goals.

The process helped heal some of their fear around money — and strengthened their bond.

**Action Step:**

Choose one small, age-appropriate financial lesson to teach your child this month.

Build from there — slowly, steadily, lovingly.

## Closing Reflection: You Are Building Stability, Hope, and Love That Will Outlive You

Raising children while grieving feels impossible some days.

But here's what you're doing — even when it feels invisible:

You are building stability where there was chaos.

You are sowing hope where there was despair.

You are teaching courage by living it in front of them every single day.

Every conversation about money.

Every trust you set up.

Every insurance form you complete.

Every budgeting decision you make.

It all says:

**I love you.**

**I believe in your future.**

**I am still fighting for us.**

You are not failing them.

You are not falling behind.

You are giving them the gift of safety.

The gift of dignity.

The gift of hope.

You are doing sacred, heroic work.

And no matter how heavy it feels some days, you are carrying it — beautifully, bravely, and with a love that will last far beyond this season.

Your children may not see it all now.

But one day, they will.

And they will say:

**He carried me.**

**He believed in me.**

**He made sure I was okay.**

One hard decision at a time.

One quiet act of courage at a time.

One unbreakable step of love at a time.

# Chapter 19: Widowers in Midlife vs Later Life

## Introduction: Different Seasons, Different Strategies

When you lose a spouse, your world splits in two: the life you had, and the life you now must build.

But the path forward — financially and emotionally — isn't the same for everyone.

**A 48-year-old widower with children still at home faces very different decisions than a 75-year-old widower entering late retirement.**

Your age, your stage of life, your financial picture — all shape what rebuilding looks like.

This chapter walks through two distinct widower journeys:

- **Midlife Widowers (40s–60s):** Rebuilding for retirement, raising kids, restarting careers.
- **Later-Life Widowers (70+):** Protecting wealth, preserving dignity, planning for legacy and care.

You'll see that both journeys are different — but neither is lesser.

Both are worthy.

Both are brave.

Both deserve careful, personalized planning.

Let's walk through them side-by-side — so you can see where you are, and how to move forward with wisdom, strength, and hope.

## Part 1: Midlife Widowers (40s–60s) — Rebuilding for Retirement

If you lost your spouse in your 40s, 50s, or early 60s, you face a unique financial and emotional challenge:

You must rebuild — while grieving.

You must plan for a future — while adjusting to a massive, painful change.

It feels unfair.

It feels overwhelming.

But it's also true:

**You still have time.**

**You still have options.**

**You still have power.**

Let's talk about what rebuilding looks like in midlife.

### *Key Priorities for Midlife Widowers:*

- Stabilizing current cash flow
- Protecting dependents (minor children, if any)
- Resuming or revising retirement savings
- Managing life insurance and Social Security benefits
- Planning for possible remarriage or blended families

### *Financial Focus #1: Stabilizing Your Immediate Needs*

Before you dream big, stabilize small.

- Review and adjust your household budget.
- Secure or maintain adequate life insurance coverage.
- Rebuild an emergency fund of 6–12 months of expenses.

- Manage any debt carefully — no rash moves.

**The goal:**

Build a calm financial foundation you can rely on.

**Real-World Example: Mike's Story**

Mike, 52, lost his wife suddenly.

At first, he wanted to quit his high-pressure job.

His advisor urged him to wait — to stabilize financially first.

Today, Mike still works — but in a less stressful role, with a growing retirement nest egg and a new plan for his 60s.

**Stabilize before you leap.**

## *Financial Focus #2: Rebuilding Retirement Savings*

Losing a spouse often derails original retirement plans.

- Two Social Security checks become one.
- Two retirement accounts become one.
- Shared expenses must be rebalanced.

**Key Midlife Retirement Moves:**

- Maximize retirement account contributions (401(k), IRA, Roth IRA).
- Catch-up contributions (if over age 50) can help rebuild faster.
- Reassess your investment strategy — you may need more growth-oriented investing, but with balanced risk.

**Pros and Cons of Aggressive Retirement Saving Post-Loss:**

**Pros:**

- Helps close retirement savings gaps.
- Regains momentum toward future security.
- Builds emotional confidence.

**Cons:**

- Requires strict budgeting and discipline now.
- Can feel overwhelming amid grief.

**Action Step:**

Review your retirement accounts within 90 days.

Set new contribution targets based on your current reality — not your old plan.

Even small increases matter.

## *Financial Focus #3: Managing Social Security and Life Insurance Payouts*

If your spouse worked and paid into Social Security, you may be eligible for survivor benefits.

**Strategies for Midlife Widowers:**

- Evaluate if you qualify for survivor benefits based on age (available as early as 60, or 50 if disabled).
- Consider delaying your own Social Security claim to maximize future payouts.

Life insurance proceeds (if received) must also be managed carefully:

- Pay off high-interest debt first.
- Preserve the rest — invest it conservatively.
- Resist emotional or impulsive spending.

**Real-World Example: Daniel's Story**

Daniel, 58, received a $500,000 life insurance payout after losing his wife.

He paid off his mortgage, boosted his retirement savings, and reserved a portion for future travel dreams.

Today, he calls that financial stability "the last gift my wife gave me."

**Action Step:**

Work with a trusted fiduciary advisor to create a **post-loss financial strategy** that balances immediate needs with long-term goals.

## Part 2: Later-Life Widowers (70+) — Focusing on Protection and Preservation

If you lost your spouse in your 70s or beyond, your financial path looks different.

You are not trying to build wealth.

You are trying to **protect** wealth.

You are not trying to race toward retirement.

You are trying to **preserve dignity and security.**

And your emotional needs — stability, peace, family connection — are more important than ever.

Let's walk through what financial rebuilding looks like in later life.

### *Key Priorities for Later-Life Widowers:*

- Ensuring steady, reliable income
- Minimizing risk to principal assets
- Simplifying financial accounts and estate documents
- Planning for healthcare, long-term care, and final expenses
- Gifting thoughtfully — not recklessly

### *Financial Focus #1: Protecting Your Income Streams*

At this stage, income predictability matters more than growth.

- Maximize Social Security survivor benefits.
- Evaluate pension survivor options if applicable.
- Use conservative withdrawal strategies for retirement accounts (e.g.,

4% rule).

- Consider annuities for guaranteed lifetime income (but only carefully — not all annuities are created equal).

**Pros and Cons of Annuities in Later Life:**

**Pros:**

- Provides steady, predictable income.
- Reduces fear of outliving assets.

**Cons:**

- Can be expensive or inflexible.
- Some annuities have complex terms or hidden fees.

**Real-World Example: George's Story**

George, 76, used part of his IRA to purchase a simple, low-cost immediate annuity —

guaranteeing a monthly check for life alongside his Social Security.

The peace of mind?

Priceless.

**Action Step:**

Review all income streams.

Prioritize **reliable cash flow** over risky investments or chasing returns.

## *Financial Focus #2: Simplifying and Securing Your Estate*

Later-life widowers should focus on:

- Consolidating financial accounts where possible.
- Naming clear, updated beneficiaries.
- Creating or reviewing wills and trusts.
- Appointing powers of attorney and healthcare proxies.

Simplicity now prevents confusion, conflict, and costs later.

**Action Step:**

Schedule an estate review with an attorney and financial advisor within 12 months of your spouse's passing.

### *Financial Focus #3: Healthcare and Long-Term Care Planning*

Later life brings new realities:

- Medicare plan reviews annually.
- Long-term care insurance evaluations or alternatives.
- Clear advance directives (living wills, DNRs, etc.).

**Real-World Example: Edward's Story**

Edward, 79, updated his healthcare directives and purchased a small final expense insurance policy.

His children said later it was the greatest kindness he ever gave them — because when the time came, they knew exactly what he wanted.

**Action Step:**

Create a written healthcare plan — even if it's just a letter — and share it with your adult children or trusted friends.

## Part 3: Different Strategies Based on Age — A Side-by-Side Summary

Midlife Widowers (40s–60s)Later-Life Widowers (70+)

**Focus**

Rebuilding, growth

Protecting, preserving

**Income**

Earnings + survivor benefits

Pensions + Social Security

**Investments**

Moderate growth strategy

Conservative income strategy

**Estate Planning**

Guardianship + trusts for kids

Simplification + healthcare planning

**Goals**

Retirement funding, stability

Dignity, peace of mind, gifting

## Closing Reflection: No Matter Your Age, Your Life Is Still Worth Building

Whether you are 48 or 78, this is true:

**You still matter.**

**Your choices still matter.**

**Your dreams still matter.**

Midlife widowers rebuild.

Later-life widowers protect.

But both are acts of fierce love and strength.

You are not too young to dream new dreams.

You are not too old to make wise, empowering choices.

You are not behind.

You are not broken.

You are right where you are supposed to be — standing on the foundation of love, building something new.

One choice at a time.

One breath at a time.

One act of hope at a time.

Your best chapters are not behind you.

They are still being written —

with courage, with care, and with a heart that refuses to give up.

# Chapter 20: Remarrying and Financial Blending

## Introduction: New Love, New Life — And New Financial Realities

When you lose a spouse, the idea of loving again can feel unimaginable.

And when it happens — quietly, slowly, bravely — it feels like a miracle.

But falling in love again doesn't erase your financial reality.

It adds to it.

Remarrying after widowhood brings deep emotional renewal.

It also brings new financial responsibilities — and new complexities.

This chapter walks you through:

- What you need to know about remarriage and money
- How pre-nuptial and post-nuptial agreements can protect both love and legacy
- Smart estate planning tips for blended families

It's not about being cynical.

It's about being wise.

It's not about protecting yourself from your new partner.

It's about protecting the love you are building — from confusion, conflict, and unintended harm.

And most of all, it's about giving yourself the freedom to build a new chapter joyfully, intentionally, and securely.

Let's take it slow, steady, and wise.

## Part 1: What to Know About Remarriage and Money

Marriage is always emotional.

But after widowhood, it's also highly financial.

### *Financial Realities of Remarrying as a Widower:*

- Your Social Security benefits may change.
- Your spouse's survivor benefits could be affected.
- Your children's future inheritance could be diluted unintentionally.
- Your new spouse's debts, obligations, or financial habits may impact you.
- Blended families can introduce complex emotional and legal dynamics.

**Why It's Different After Widowhood:**

Unlike a first marriage — where two people build from scratch — remarriage often involves:

- Established assets
- Adult or minor children
- Prior promises made to late spouses
- Emotional baggage around money, death, and loyalty

It's a beautiful, complicated tapestry.

And it deserves careful, loving thought.

**Real-World Example: Bill's Story**

Bill, 68, fell in love again five years after losing his wife.

Before marrying, he and his fiancée worked with financial and legal advisors.

They updated wills, established separate bank accounts, and created a trust to ensure Bill's children still inherited fairly.

It wasn't unromantic.

It was respectful — to each other, and to the families they loved.

**Action Step:**

Before remarrying, schedule a meeting with a financial planner and an estate attorney.

Map out your new financial reality clearly — before rings are exchanged.

## Part 2: Pre-Nups and Post-Nups for Widowers — Not Just for the Wealthy

The words "pre-nuptial agreement" can feel uncomfortable.

Maybe even cold.

But when you're remarrying after loss — especially with adult children, complex assets, or significant savings —

a **pre-nup** or **post-nup** can be one of the greatest acts of love and clarity you give your new marriage.

### *What is a Pre-Nuptial Agreement?*

A **pre-nuptial agreement** is a legal contract signed before marriage outlining:

- What assets remain separate
- How assets would be divided in divorce
- Financial expectations during the marriage
- Protection of children's inheritance rights

### *What is a Post-Nuptial Agreement?*

A **post-nuptial agreement** is similar — but signed **after** the marriage has already taken place.

Both tools protect both spouses — not from each other, but from future confusion, conflict, or unintended harm.

### *Why Widowers Should Strongly Consider One:*

- Protects assets intended for children or grandchildren.
- Clarifies which assets are shared and which are separate.
- Reduces financial anxiety or resentment in blended family situations.
- Provides peace of mind for you and your new spouse.

**Pros and Cons of Pre-Nups/Post-Nups:**

**Pros:**

- Prevents family disputes after death.
- Preserves intended inheritance.
- Provides clarity and fairness up front.

**Cons:**

- Emotional difficulty discussing finances.
- Legal costs to draft properly.

**Real-World Example: Tom's Story**

Tom, 62, remarried after losing his wife of 40 years.

His pre-nup:

- Preserved his home and retirement accounts for his two daughters.
- Ensured his new wife had guaranteed access to health insurance, living expenses, and a jointly-owned vacation property.

Both families felt respected.

No secrets.

No surprises.

**Action Step:**

Have an open, respectful conversation about a pre-nup or post-nup with your future spouse.

Frame it as an act of mutual protection, not mistrust.

Then work with a qualified attorney to create a document that honors both of you.

## Part 3: Blended Family Estate Planning Tips — Keeping Love and Legacy Balanced

Blended families are beautiful —

but they can also be **financial minefields** if not handled with care.

When adult children, stepchildren, and new spouses are all involved, estate planning becomes even more important — and more delicate.

### *Smart Strategies for Blended Family Estate Planning:*

**1. Update Wills and Trusts Immediately**

If you die without updating your estate plan, state laws may:

- Give everything to your new spouse
- Disinherit your children
- Create conflict among survivors

**Updated documents are non-negotiable.**

**2. Consider a QTIP Trust**

A **Qualified Terminable Interest Property (QTIP) Trust**:

- Provides income for your surviving spouse during their lifetime
- Preserves the principal for your children after the spouse's death

**Win-win** when you want to care for both spouse and children.

**3. Use Life Insurance Thoughtfully**

- Life insurance can provide for a new spouse —
- without touching assets intended for children.
- It can also equalize inheritances among stepchildren and biological children.

**4. Clarify Beneficiary Designations**

- Retirement accounts (401(k)s, IRAs)
- Life insurance policies
- Bank accounts

These assets **pass outside your will** —
so updating beneficiaries is essential.

**5. Communicate Openly with Family**

Silence breeds suspicion.
Transparency builds trust.
You don't have to share every dollar amount —
but sharing intentions now can prevent heartbreak later.

**Real-World Example: David's Story**

David, 74, remarried a widow with two adult sons.
He updated his will to leave personal property and specific financial gifts to his children —
while ensuring his wife had lifetime use of their home.
Both sides of the blended family knew the plan ahead of time.
There were tears — but also peace.

**Action Step:**

After remarrying, meet with an estate planning attorney immediately.
Create or update your will, trusts, and all beneficiary designations to reflect your new blended family reality.

## Closing Reflection: Love Deserves Both Heart and Wisdom

It's easy to think:

"If we love each other enough, everything will work out."
But true love — especially after the loss you've endured —
deserves both passion and planning.
Emotion and structure.
Heart and wisdom.
Remarrying is a beautiful act of hope.
Blending finances thoughtfully is an act of deep, practical love —
for your new spouse,
for your children,
for yourself.
You don't honor your late spouse by living in fear.
You honor them — and yourself — by living fully, wisely, and bravely.
You have a right to dream again.
To build again.
To love again.
And you have a right to protect what you are building —
so that it lasts,
blesses everyone you care about,
and stands strong no matter what life brings next.
One conversation at a time.
One plan at a time.
One act of wise, courageous love at a time.
You are not closing the book on your past.
You are writing a new chapter —
full of dignity, hope, strength, and light.

# Closing Chapter 21: Healing Takes Time — So Does Financial Healing

## Introduction: Two Journeys, One Heart

Grief and financial rebuilding feel like two separate journeys.

One tugs at your heart.

The other tugs at your mind.

One is invisible and chaotic.

The other is practical and structured.

But if you look closer, you'll see:

**They are the same journey.**

**Two parts of the same whole.**

**Two expressions of the same deep, unbreakable love.**

You are not just healing emotionally.

You are healing financially.

And both take time.

This closing chapter is your reminder:

- You are not "behind."
- You are not "failing."
- You are doing something extraordinary.

You are rebuilding your life — heart and wallet alike — one day, one breath, one wise choice at a time.

Let's walk through this final chapter together — steady, strong, proud.

## Part 1: Grief and Financial Rebuilding Are Parallel Journeys

It's easy to think:

"I should have figured this out by now."

"I should be stronger by now."

"I should have handled all this paperwork by now."

But grief doesn't follow a calendar.

And neither does financial healing.

They move together — slow, steady, nonlinear.

### *How Grief and Financial Recovery Mirror Each Other:*

Grief Journey Financial Healing Journey

Sudden waves of emotion

Unexpected financial decisions

Overwhelm and paralysis

Paperwork and legal complexities

Small wins (a day without tears)

Small wins (updating a will)

Setbacks (birthdays, anniversaries)

Setbacks (unexpected expenses)

Gradual growth in resilience

Gradual growth in confidence

New understanding of self

New understanding of finances

Both journeys:

- Require patience.
- Require forgiveness.
- Require compassion for yourself.

**Real-World Example: John's Story**

John, 59, thought he'd "handle everything" quickly after his wife passed. But he found himself emotionally frozen — unable to call banks, unwilling to open financial statements.

Only after giving himself permission to move at his own pace did he start making progress —

one phone call, one form, one small decision at a time.

**Action Step:**

Write this down and post it somewhere visible:

*"I am rebuilding my life — and that takes courage, not speed."*

## Part 2: You're Not "Behind" — You're Healing at Your Own Pace

Comparison is poison.

Maybe you know another widower who sold the house in six months.

Maybe you know someone who remarried within a year.

Maybe you know someone who seems to have "bounced back" faster.

It doesn't matter.

You are not them.

Your journey is yours.

### *Common Guilt Traps Widowers Face:*

- "I should have gone through the papers by now."
- "I should have known how the life insurance worked."
- "I shouldn't be spending this money — or I should be spending it differently."
- "I should have a new plan by now."

Let's rewrite those lies:

- "I'm learning, not failing."
- "I'm making thoughtful decisions when I'm ready."
- "I honor my spouse best by taking care of myself with patience and respect."

**Real-World Example: Henry's Story**

Henry, 70, spent almost two years before updating all his financial accounts after his wife's death.

When he finally did, he said:

*"It took me that long because I needed that long. And that's okay."*

**Action Step:**

When guilt arises, replace it with gratitude.

Instead of:

*"I'm behind."*

Say:

*"I am healing at the speed of love."*

## Part 3: Financial Strength Is Self-Care

It's easy to separate "grief work" from "financial work" in your mind.

But they are connected.

Taking care of your financial life is an act of self-respect.

An act of self-love.

An act of stability.

And stability is part of healing.

### *Why Financial Strength Matters After Loss:*

- It reduces anxiety.
- It increases options for the future.
- It models resilience for your children and grandchildren.
- It gives you the dignity of choice, not desperation.

Money can't fix grief.

But financial stability can make grief gentler.

It can give you breathing room to heal emotionally — without the added burden of crisis or chaos.

**Real-World Example: Martin's Story**

Martin, 65, created a simple new budget six months after losing his wife.

He said:

> *"It wasn't about the money. It was about knowing I could survive this — financially and emotionally."*

**Action Step:**

Reframe financial tasks as self-care, not chores.

Updating your will?

**Self-care.**

Building a savings cushion?

**Self-care.**

Meeting with a financial planner?

**Self-care.**

You are not just managing money.

You are nurturing your future self.

## Part 4: Final Checklist — The Year After Loss

No two widowers walk the same timeline.

But generally, within the first 12–18 months after loss, most widowers benefit from addressing:

### *Legal and Estate Planning:*

- Update will and trust documents.
- Update powers of attorney and healthcare proxies.
- Confirm and update beneficiary designations on retirement accounts and life insurance.
- Review real estate titles and deeds.

### *Banking and Financial Accounts:*

- Retitle or close joint bank accounts as needed.
- Set up accounts in your name only.
- Review all automatic payments and stop unnecessary ones.
- Consolidate scattered accounts when appropriate.

### *Insurance:*

- Review life insurance needs (for yourself and any dependents).
- Update property and casualty insurance (homeowners, auto).
- Evaluate long-term care insurance options if age-appropriate.

### *Income and Cash Flow:*

- Apply for Social Security survivor benefits if eligible.
- Review pensions, annuities, and income streams.
- Create a new monthly and annual budget.

*Investments:*

- Reassess your investment strategy based on new goals and risk tolerance.
- Review inherited accounts and required minimum distributions (RMDs) if applicable.
- Consider working with a fiduciary financial advisor for ongoing planning.

*Taxes:*

- Understand your tax filing status changes (e.g., "Qualifying Widow(er)" for two years after loss).
- Coordinate with a CPA familiar with grief-aware financial transitions.

*Emotional and Practical Preparation:*

- Begin legacy planning (letter to heirs, final wishes).
- Consider charitable giving or scholarships in honor of your spouse.
- Give yourself permission to dream again — travel, hobbies, new experiences.

**Action Step:**

Pick ONE item from the checklist each month.
Small steps build big futures.

## Closing Reflection: Healing Is Not a Race. It's a Testament of Love.

You have survived something most people fear even thinking about.

You have walked through unimaginable grief.

You have faced overwhelming decisions.

You have kept going — even on days when you didn't think you could.

And now?

You are not just surviving.

You are healing.

Emotionally.

Financially.

Spiritually.

It is not easy.

It is not fast.

But it is sacred.

You are honoring your past.

You are surviving your present.

You are building your future.

One breath.

One choice.

One beautiful, defiant act of hope at a time.

You are proof:

That love endures.

That strength is quiet and steady.

That new life grows from deep loss.

Your spouse would be proud of you.

You should be proud of you.

And your future?

It's still bright.

Still possible.

Still waiting for you to step into it — with wisdom, courage, and love.

Healing takes time.

Financial healing takes time.
And you, brave soul, are right on time.

# About the Author

Patrick Brown, MBA, is a financial advisor, educator, and advocate for those rebuilding their lives after profound loss—especially widowers. With over two decades of experience in wealth management, retirement planning, insurance, and financial literacy, Patrick brings more than just credentials to his work—he brings heart.

His passion for financial education began on a deeply personal level. After witnessing the impact of financial confusion, grief, and emotional overwhelm within his own family and community, Patrick made it his mission to become a trustworthy, relatable voice in the world of personal finance.

Patrick is the founder of multiple financial education platforms, including *Financial Literacy for Widowers*, created to serve the unique and often overlooked needs of those navigating life after the death of a spouse. Through this book and others in his growing financial literacy series, he empowers people to take back control of their financial lives, rebuild with intention, and write a new chapter filled with dignity, clarity, and hope.

A former Division I athlete and CFL football player turned trusted financial professional, Patrick combines discipline with compassion. He knows what it's like to face unexpected life transitions—and what it takes to move forward with strength and purpose.

Today, Patrick continues to guide individuals and families through every season of life, offering steady mentorship, practical tools, and the kind of financial wisdom that doesn't just teach—it heals.

When he's not writing or advising, Patrick enjoys family time with his wife and daughters, community service, public speaking, and inspiring others to take the next right step—financially, personally, and with courage.

# Should You Work with a Financial Advisor?

**Understanding the Pros, Cons, and What Makes Sense for You**

Losing your spouse doesn't just leave you carrying emotional grief—it often means carrying financial responsibilities alone for the first time in years, or even decades.

Between budgeting, retirement planning, insurance updates, tax filings, and estate decisions, it can be hard to know what to prioritize or how to put the pieces back together.

For many widowers, hiring a financial advisor can offer structure, clarity, and much-needed peace of mind.

But it's not the right choice for everyone—and that's okay.

The key is understanding what an advisor does, what it costs, and whether it fits your needs and goals right now.

Let's walk through it together.

## Pros of Working with a Financial Advisor

### *1. Guidance Across All the Moving Parts*

A qualified financial advisor can help with everything from restructuring your retirement strategy to understanding tax implications after your spouse's passing.

They can assist you with retitling accounts, reviewing insurance needs, updating beneficiaries, handling investment decisions, and managing the emotional side of money—all in one place.

When life feels overwhelming, a steady financial partner can bring clarity and order.

### *2. Saves Time and Reduces Stress*

When you're grieving, decision fatigue is real.

A financial advisor can take complex tasks off your plate and simplify choices, so you can focus your energy on your healing, your family, and your future—not paperwork and second-guessing.

### *3. Helps You Avoid Emotional Mistakes*

Financial decisions made in panic, grief, or loneliness can have long-term consequences.

A trusted advisor acts as a steady voice of reason—helping you stay grounded, avoid impulsive decisions, and stick to a plan that reflects your true goals, not just today's emotions.

### *4. Keeps You Accountable*

Life after loss can feel chaotic.

A financial advisor can help keep you organized and moving forward—reminding you to update documents, stay on track with savings, and complete important financial steps even when life feels heavy.

### *5. Customized, Personal Planning*

Grieving is personal.

Widowhood is personal.

And your financial plan should be too.

A good advisor tailors everything to your unique situation: your income, assets, debts, family dynamics, future dreams, and the promises you want to keep to your spouse and yourself.

## Cons of Working with a Financial Advisor

### *1. There's a Cost*

Advisors typically charge a percentage of assets under management (usually 0.5%–1%), a flat fee, or hourly rates.

If your finances are tight after your loss—or if your situation is relatively simple—you may feel that the cost outweighs the benefit right now.

### *2. Quality Varies (A Lot)*

Not all financial advisors are fiduciaries (meaning, legally required to act in your best interest).

Some work on commissions tied to the products they sell.

It's important to ask clear questions:

- Are you a fiduciary?
- How are you compensated?
- Will you put my interests first?

### *3. You Still Need to Be Involved*

Hiring an advisor isn't handing over the reins entirely.

Your goals, values, and input are essential.

Think of it like hiring a personal trainer: they can guide, but you still have to show up and do the work.

### *4. Risk of Cookie-Cutter Advice*

Some advisors use generic templates or prepackaged strategies that may not fully fit your life now.

Widowers face unique challenges—grief, sudden solo retirement, blended family concerns—that require more thoughtful, customized planning.

### *5. DIY May Be Enough for Some*

If you enjoy learning about finances, your needs are fairly straightforward, and you're comfortable managing budgets, investments, and paperwork, you might do just fine using online tools and resources.

Today's apps, calculators, and budgeting templates make DIY financial management more accessible than ever.

## So... Should You Hire a Financial Advisor?

Here are a few questions to help you decide:

- Do you feel overwhelmed about where to start financially?
- Are you juggling multiple accounts, insurance updates, or estate issues?
- Do you have children, business interests, or real estate that complicate decisions?
- Do you want someone experienced to walk this financial journey with you—so you don't have to figure it all out alone?

If you answered yes to any of these,

**a financial advisor could be a worthwhile investment in your peace of mind.**

## Final Thought: You Deserve a Plan—and a Partner

You've already walked through one of life's hardest chapters.

You've survived what many people fear even imagining.

You deserve a financial future that feels steady, intentional, and supportive of who you are now—not who you used to be.

A good financial advisor won't just hand you spreadsheets or pitch investments.

They'll offer perspective.

They'll rebuild confidence.

They'll stand beside you as you take control of your next chapter—one steady decision at a time.

And if you're not ready to work with an advisor just yet?

That's okay too.

You're still moving forward.

You're still healing.

You're doing better than you think.

And your financial life?

It's still full of possibility, hope, and strength.

You are building something beautiful.

# Disclaimer

A Note to the Reader: Understanding the Purpose and Limits of This Book

*Financial Literacy for Widowers* was written to educate, empower, and encourage individuals navigating the emotional and financial complexities of life after the death of a spouse.

The insights in this book are based on the author's personal experiences, professional training, and over two decades of work in financial services, personal development, and educational outreach.

That said, it's important to clarify what this book is—and what it is not.

## For Educational Purposes Only

This book is intended solely for general educational and informational purposes.

It is designed to provide widowers with foundational financial knowledge, tools for responsible decision-making, and awareness of common challenges and opportunities in life after loss.

While this book includes strategies, case examples, and financial principles, it does **not** constitute personalized financial advice.

Every reader's financial journey is unique.

Your income, assets, debts, family structure, tax situation, health needs, and long-term goals will differ significantly from those of others.

Before making any major financial, legal, or business decisions, you should consult directly with qualified professionals licensed to provide tailored advice based on your personal circumstances.

## No Legal Advice

Although this book touches on legal topics often involved after the death of a spouse—such as probate, estate planning, beneficiary designations, and powers of attorney—it does **not** constitute legal advice.

It is **not** a substitute for working with a licensed attorney.

If you are:

- Administering or settling an estate
- Updating or creating a will or trust
- Navigating probate or non-probate asset transfers
- Managing guardianship issues for minor children
- Addressing real estate titles, deeds, or survivorship rights

...you should seek legal counsel from an attorney who specializes in estate planning, elder law, or probate matters in your state.

Laws vary widely based on jurisdiction and circumstances.

Only a licensed attorney can ensure that your legal rights and responsibilities are protected properly.

## No Financial or Investment Advice

This book is not authored by a Certified Financial Planner™, Registered Investment Advisor, or licensed broker-dealer.

While it offers ideas, frameworks, and general financial strategies, it does **not** provide personalized investment recommendations, individualized financial planning, or securities advice.

If you are considering:

- Investing proceeds from insurance payouts, retirement accounts, or estate distributions
- Developing a new retirement withdrawal plan
- Rebalancing investment portfolios after a spouse's passing

- Making changes to insurance contracts or annuity plans
- Planning for gifting or charitable giving

...you should work with a licensed financial professional who can evaluate your personal financial situation and goals.

No outcomes are guaranteed.

Investments involve risk, and all readers are ultimately responsible for their own financial decisions.

## No Accounting or Tax Advice

Although taxes often play a major role after the loss of a spouse—affecting income taxes, estate taxes, Social Security benefits, and investment accounts—this book is **not** authored by a CPA, enrolled agent, or licensed tax preparer.

If you:

- Need help understanding the tax impact of survivor benefits, estate transfers, or retirement account rollovers
- Are filing taxes for the first time as a single filer or surviving spouse
- Receive income from multiple sources or states
- Own businesses, real estate, or investment properties
- Are managing required minimum distributions (RMDs)

...you should consult a licensed tax professional who can ensure your filings are correct, compliant, and optimized for your situation.

Any discussion of tax concepts in this book is for general awareness purposes only.

## No Guarantees or Promises

Reading this book does not guarantee financial success, wealth accumulation, or personal peace.

Every individual's circumstances, choices, behaviors, and outcomes are different.

Any case studies, examples, or numbers presented are meant to illustrate concepts—not to predict actual results or imply specific financial outcomes.

Progress after the death of a spouse is deeply personal.

What worked for one person may not work for another.

The goal of this book is to empower you with knowledge, clarity, and practical tools—not to offer one-size-fits-all solutions.

## Limitation of Liability

By reading this book, you agree that the author, Patrick Brown, MBA, and all affiliated platforms—including *FinancialLiteracyForWidowers.com* and related brands—are not responsible for any financial decisions, outcomes, or consequences that may result from the use of the information presented.

The author and affiliated entities expressly disclaim liability for any financial losses, legal disputes, tax issues, or other personal or business impacts connected to the content of this book.

You are solely responsible for your financial choices.

## Build a Support Team

The author believes strongly that every widower deserves access to a trustworthy team of professionals—

including a financial advisor, estate attorney, tax professional, insurance consultant, and if needed, a therapist or grief counselor.

This book is designed to **complement** that professional team—not replace it.

If you haven't yet built your team, consider this your invitation to begin.

Financial healing, like emotional healing, is not a solo journey.

You've already survived one of life's greatest losses.

Now it's time to rebuild your financial life with the same resilience, care, and dignity that helped you survive the storm.

Your next chapter is still being written—and it can be full of wisdom, peace, and strength.

You are not just surviving.

You are leading yourself, and those who love you, toward a future built on courage, compassion, and intentional growth.

And that is a victory worth celebrating.

# A Month-by-Month Guide to Staying Organized, Empowered, and Proactive

When you're managing money on your own—possibly for the first time in decades—it can feel like you're always trying to catch up.

There's paperwork, deadlines, taxes, insurance, and investment accounts that suddenly rest on your shoulders alone.

This financial calendar is designed to help you stay ahead—without overwhelm.

Each month brings key tasks, reminders, and simple planning moments to keep your finances healthy, your documents in order, and your stress levels lower.

Let's take it one step at a time.

This isn't about perfection.

It's about consistency, confidence, and clarity as you move forward into your next chapter.

## JANUARY

### January 1

- New contribution limits go into effect for 401(k), 403(b), 457 plans, IRAs, and Roth IRAs.
- HSA and FSA limits reset—review and adjust your contributions if needed.
- Begin the year with a fresh budget and cash flow review.
- Update paycheck withholding (Form W-4) if your filing status or

income changed after your spouse's passing.

**January 15**

- 4th Quarter Estimated Taxes Due for prior year income (October–December). Use IRS Form 1040-ES if applicable.

**Late January**

- W-2s, 1099-NEC, 1099-MISC, 1099-INT, 1099-DIV, and 1099-Bs begin arriving from employers, banks, and brokerage firms.

## FEBRUARY

**February 1**

- Deadline for employers and payers to issue W-2s and 1099s.

**Mid to Late February**

- K-1s from partnerships or S-corps may arrive (some come later).
- Begin gathering and organizing all your tax documents or upload them to your CPA or tax preparer.

## MARCH

**March 15**

- Partnership and S-Corp tax returns due (Forms 1065 or 1120-S).
- File an extension using IRS Form 7004 if needed.

**March 31**

- Deadline to receive electronic Forms 1095-A/B/C (proof of health insurance).

## APRIL

### April 1

- If you turned 73 last year and delayed your first Required Minimum Distribution (RMD), today is your deadline to take it.

### April 15 (or next business day)

- Personal Tax Filing Deadline (IRS Form 1040).
- 1st Quarter Estimated Taxes Due.
- Last day to make prior-year contributions to:
- Traditional or Roth IRA
- SEP IRA (unless extended)
- HSA (Health Savings Account)
- Coverdell ESA
- Deadline to file for an extension (IRS Form 4868).
- FAFSA deadlines apply in some states if helping children or grandchildren with college planning.

## MAY

### Early May

- Review your property tax assessment. Protest deadlines usually fall mid-month, depending on your state.

### May 29 — National 529 Day

- Review or open a 529 College Savings Plan for children or grandchildren.

## JUNE

### June 15

- 2nd Quarter Estimated Taxes Due.
- U.S. citizens living abroad: deadline to file federal tax returns (automatic extension to October 15 available).

### Mid-June

- Mid-year retirement account check-in: review performance, adjust contributions if necessary.
- Revisit charitable giving plans for the year.

## JULY

### July 1–15

- Mid-Year Financial Check-In:
- Revisit your new solo budget and adjust if needed.
- Review debt payoff progress.
- Rebalance your investment portfolio if allocations have shifted by more than 5–10%.
- Schedule a mid-year review with your financial advisor.

## AUGUST

### August 1–31

- Start preparing for fall open enrollment.
- Review your HSA and FSA balances.

- Revisit insurance coverages: life, disability, umbrella, long-term care.
- Begin planning for year-end charitable giving (especially if considering Donor-Advised Funds or Qualified Charitable Distributions if age 70½+).

## SEPTEMBER

### September 15

- 3rd Quarter Estimated Taxes Due.
- Deadline for extended tax filings for Partnerships and S-Corporations.

### Late September

- Consider tax-loss harvesting strategies if needed.
- Review Roth conversion opportunities before year-end.

## OCTOBER

### October 1

- Deadline to establish a SIMPLE IRA for the current tax year.
- Medicare Open Enrollment Preview window opens (important if you're age 65+ or assisting an aging parent).

### October 15

- Final deadline to file extended individual tax returns (Form 1040).
- Final deadline to fund prior-year SEP IRAs (if extended).
- Deadline to recharacterize a Roth IRA contribution if correcting.

### Late October

- Employer open enrollment period: review health plan options, life/disability insurance, and benefits.

## NOVEMBER

### November 1–30

- ACA Health Insurance Open Enrollment opens.
- Employer open enrollment finalizes—finalize elections for:
- Health plans
- HSA or FSA contributions
- Life, disability, or supplemental insurance
- 401(k) deferral changes

### Black Friday/Cyber Monday Weekend

- Make year-end purchase decisions wisely: business expenses, technology upgrades, charitable gifts.

## DECEMBER

### December 1–15

- Final push to maximize:
- 401(k), 403(b), 457 contributions
- HSA contributions
- Roth conversions (if part of your plan)
- Charitable giving deductions

### December 31 – Year-End Deadlines

- Take RMDs if age 73+.
- Complete any Roth IRA conversions.

- Finalize tax-loss harvesting.
- Make final charitable contributions (cash, appreciated stock, DAFs).
- Maximize gifting ($18,000 per person in 2024 for the annual gift tax exclusion).
- Spend down Flexible Spending Accounts (FSAs) if applicable.

## Rolling and Event-Based Reminders

### Every Paycheck

- Verify correct 401(k) deductions.
- Confirm health, dental, and HSA payroll deductions.

### After Major Life Events

- Update financial accounts, legal documents, and beneficiary designations after:
- Marriage or remarriage
- Birth or adoption of grandchildren
- Receiving an inheritance
- Major health changes

### Quarterly

- Review your budget and spending habits.
- Make quarterly estimated tax payments if needed.
- Rebalance investments if drifted from targets.
- Meet with your advisor if doing complex tax planning.

## Final Tip: Automate What You Can

Set calendar reminders.

Automate retirement contributions.

Use auto-pay for bills.

Keep a running list of financial tasks by month or quarter.

Life after loss can feel unpredictable.

But your financial world doesn't have to.

The more structure you build, the more peace you'll create.

You don't have to manage everything at once.

You just need to keep showing up—month by month, choice by choice, step by step.

You are doing far better than you think.

And your future is still very much in your hands.

# 100 questions a widower should consider asking financial advisors, CPAs, attorneys, professionals

**Financial Advisor Questions**

1. Are you a fiduciary at all times when working with me?
2. How are you compensated—fee-only, commission, or a mix?
3. What services do you provide beyond investment management?
4. Do you specialize in working with widowed clients?
5. How will you help me rebuild my financial plan after my spouse's passing?
6. Can you help me with budgeting and cash flow planning?
7. Will you review my insurance policies?
8. How will you help me with Social Security decisions?
9. Do you provide retirement income planning?
10. Can you assist with estate planning coordination?
11. How do you manage investment risk for clients in transition?
12. Will you educate me as we go, or just manage investments?
13. What is your investment philosophy?
14. What happens if something happens to you? Is there a backup advisor?
15. How often will we meet or review my plan?
16. Can you help me understand Required Minimum Distributions (RMDs)?
17. What happens if I need to access my investments sooner than planned?
18. How do you help widowed clients avoid scams?

19. Will you help me update beneficiary designations?
20. How do you ensure my financial plan adapts if my circumstances change?

**CPA or Tax Professional Questions**

1. How do I file taxes the year my spouse passed away?
2. Am I eligible for Qualifying Widow(er) filing status?
3. How does my Social Security income affect my taxes now?
4. Will I owe estate taxes or inheritance taxes?
5. Can you help me plan my estimated taxes now that my situation has changed?
6. What documents do I need to keep for tax purposes after my spouse's death?
7. How should I handle taxes on insurance payouts?
8. Do I need to worry about capital gains when selling the house?
9. How will selling or transferring assets impact my tax bracket?
10. Should I adjust my tax withholding on pensions, annuities, or Social Security?
11. Can I still contribute to retirement accounts?
12. Should I consider a Roth conversion now?
13. How will my RMDs change after my spouse's passing?
14. What is the tax impact of inherited IRAs?
15. Are there any special deductions widowers qualify for?
16. Can you help me evaluate charitable giving strategies for tax savings?
17. How will remarriage impact my tax situation if it happens?
18. What tax documents should I expect to receive after my spouse's death?
19. Do I need to amend any prior-year tax returns?
20. Can you help me understand state-specific tax obligations?

**Attorney (Estate, Probate, Elder Law) Questions**

1. Do I need to open a probate case for my spouse's estate?

2. What assets are probate and what are non-probate?
3. How do I transfer ownership of real estate after my spouse's death?
4. How do I update the title on vehicles and personal property?
5. How do I handle bank accounts held jointly with my spouse?
6. Should I create a new will or trust?
7. Do I need to update my power of attorney documents?
8. Should I update my healthcare directives?
9. What estate planning documents need immediate attention?
10. How do I protect my assets if I remarry?
11. Can you explain what a revocable living trust is and whether I need one?
12. Should I consider a special needs trust for any dependents?
13. What steps can I take to minimize probate costs for my heirs?
14. How can I ensure my children or beneficiaries inherit according to my wishes?
15. What happens if I become incapacitated in the future?
16. How do I make sure my life insurance payout is handled properly in my estate?
17. Can you help me appoint a new executor or trustee?
18. How do I handle digital assets (online accounts, cryptocurrencies, etc.) in my estate plan?
19. How can I protect my estate from potential creditors?
20. What happens if I move to a different state—does my estate plan need to change?

**Insurance Professional Questions**

1. Do I need to change my life insurance coverage now?
2. Should I purchase long-term care insurance?
3. How do I update beneficiaries on existing policies?
4. Are there life insurance policies I need to claim that I may have missed?
5. Should I consider disability insurance if I'm still working?
6. How do I evaluate whether I need an umbrella insurance policy?

7. Does my homeowner's insurance need to be updated after my spouse's death?
8. Should I review my auto insurance coverage?
9. What happens to any policies that were in my spouse's name?
10. Are there accidental death and dismemberment benefits I should be aware of?

**Banker or Credit Union Officer Questions**

1. How do I remove my deceased spouse's name from joint accounts?
2. What happens to joint safe deposit boxes?
3. How do I retitle certificates of deposit (CDs) or savings bonds?
4. Can I get a certified copy of my spouse's signature history if needed?
5. Are there any special financial services for widowers that I should consider?
6. Can I simplify or consolidate my banking relationships?
7. Do I need to open a new trust or estate account?
8. What fraud protections should I add to my accounts now?
9. How do I ensure my recurring bills are properly updated to my name?
10. How do I close or transfer credit cards that were in both our names?

**Social Security Representative Questions**

1. Am I eligible for survivor benefits from Social Security?
2. Should I take survivor benefits now or delay them?
3. How does claiming survivor benefits impact my own retirement benefits later?
4. If I remarry, how will it affect my survivor benefits?
5. Can I switch from survivor benefits to my own work record later?
6. How are Social Security benefits taxed now?
7. Can I claim benefits for any dependent children still living with me?
8. How do I apply for the one-time Social Security death benefit?
9. How long does it typically take for survivor benefits to start?

10. Can you explain my options if I'm disabled or become disabled later?

**Other Professional or Practical Questions**

1. Should I hire a grief-aware financial coach or counselor?
2. Are there financial literacy programs specifically for widowers?
3. How do I protect myself from scams targeting widowed individuals?
4. Should I sign up for credit monitoring now?
5. What steps should I take to protect my digital identity?
6. Is there a checklist for closing or memorializing social media accounts?
7. How do I organize my financial documents for my family going forward?
8. Should I create a "Letter of Instruction" for my heirs?
9. How often should I review my financial plan as a widower?
10. What are the most common financial mistakes widowers make—and how can I avoid them?

# list of 100 financial, tax, mortgage, insurance, and estate planning terms

1. **Asset** – Anything you own that has value, such as cash, property, or investments.
2. **Liability** – A financial obligation or debt you owe to someone else.
3. **Net Worth** – The total value of your assets minus your liabilities.
4. **Budget** – A plan for managing your income and expenses.
5. **Cash Flow** – The movement of money into and out of your accounts.
6. **Emergency Fund** – Savings set aside for unexpected expenses or emergencies.
7. **Estate** – Everything you own at the time of your death, including property, investments, and debts.
8. **Will** – A legal document that outlines how you want your assets distributed after your death.
9. **Trust** – A legal arrangement allowing a third party to manage assets on behalf of beneficiaries.
10. **Executor** – The person responsible for carrying out the instructions in a will.
11. **Probate** – The legal process of validating a will and distributing assets after death.
12. **Beneficiary** – A person or entity entitled to receive assets from a will, trust, or financial account.
13. **Power of Attorney** – A document that gives someone authority to act on your behalf legally and financially.
14. **Advance Healthcare Directive** – A document outlining your medical

care preferences if you can't communicate.

15. **Survivor Benefits** – Payments or financial support available to the spouse or dependents of a deceased person.
16. **Required Minimum Distribution (RMD)** – The minimum amount you must withdraw annually from retirement accounts after a certain age.
17. **IRA (Individual Retirement Account)** – A tax-advantaged account for retirement savings.
18. **Roth IRA** – A retirement account where contributions are made after-tax, but withdrawals are tax-free.
19. **401(k)** – An employer-sponsored retirement savings plan allowing pre-tax contributions.
20. **Inherited IRA** – An IRA left to a beneficiary after the account owner's death.
21. **Spousal IRA Rollover** – A surviving spouse moves inherited IRA assets into their own IRA.
22. **Social Security** – A federal program providing retirement, disability, and survivor benefits.
23. **Widow(er) Benefits** – Social Security payments available to the surviving spouse based on the deceased's earnings record.
24. **Annuity** – A contract with an insurance company that provides regular income payments.
25. **Life Insurance** – A policy that pays a lump sum to beneficiaries upon the insured's death.
26. **Term Life Insurance** – Life insurance that provides coverage for a specific period.
27. **Whole Life Insurance** – Life insurance with coverage for life and a cash value component.
28. **Group Life Insurance** – Life insurance offered through an employer or organization.
29. **Death Benefit** – The money paid out from a life insurance policy upon death.
30. **Premium** – The amount you pay for insurance coverage.

31. **Estate Tax** – A tax on the transfer of a deceased person's estate.
32. **Inheritance Tax** – A tax paid by a person who inherits money or property.
33. **Capital Gains Tax** – A tax on the profit from selling an asset.
34. **Cost Basis** – The original value of an asset, used to determine taxable gains or losses.
35. **Step-Up in Basis** – A tax rule that adjusts the value of inherited assets to the current market value.
36. **Gift Tax** – A federal tax on large transfers of money or property made during your lifetime.
37. **Annual Gift Tax Exclusion** – The amount you can gift each year without paying gift tax.
38. **Tax Deduction** – An amount you can subtract from your taxable income.
39. **Tax Credit** – A dollar-for-dollar reduction of your tax liability.
40. **Form 1040** – The IRS form used for individual income tax returns.
41. **Form 1099** – A tax form reporting income earned outside of traditional employment.
42. **Form W-2** – A tax form showing wages and taxes withheld from employment.
43. **Form SSA-1099** – A tax form showing Social Security benefits received.
44. **Estimated Taxes** – Quarterly payments made to the IRS on income not subject to withholding.
45. **Extension** – An official request to delay filing your tax return.
46. **Filing Status** – Your tax category, such as Single, Married, or Qualifying Widow(er).
47. **Qualifying Widow(er)** – A special tax filing status for two years after a spouse's death.
48. **Adjusted Gross Income (AGI)** – Your total income minus certain deductions.
49. **Standard Deduction** – A flat amount the IRS allows you to deduct instead of itemizing.

50. **Itemized Deductions** – Specific expenses you can deduct instead of taking the standard deduction.
51. **Mortgage** – A loan used to purchase real estate.
52. **Principal** – The original amount of money borrowed on a loan.
53. **Interest** – The cost of borrowing money, expressed as a percentage.
54. **Escrow** – Money held by a third party for property taxes and insurance on a mortgage.
55. **Refinancing** – Replacing an existing loan with a new one, typically to get better terms.
56. **HELOC (Home Equity Line of Credit)** – A loan using the equity in your home as collateral.
57. **Reverse Mortgage** – A loan for homeowners 62 or older, allowing them to convert home equity into income.
58. **Deed** – A legal document showing ownership of property.
59. **Title** – The legal right to own and use property.
60. **Property Tax** – A tax paid to local government based on the value of your real estate.
61. **Umbrella Insurance** – Extra liability insurance protecting assets beyond standard policies.
62. **Long-Term Care Insurance** – Insurance covering expenses related to extended medical care needs.
63. **Health Savings Account (HSA)** – A tax-advantaged savings account for healthcare expenses.
64. **Flexible Spending Account (FSA)** – A pre-tax savings account for medical or dependent care expenses.
65. **Medicare** – Federal health insurance for people 65 and older or with certain disabilities.
66. **Medicare Part A** – Hospital insurance.
67. **Medicare Part B** – Medical insurance for outpatient care.
68. **Medicare Part D** – Prescription drug coverage.
69. **Medigap Policy** – Private insurance that covers costs Medicare doesn't fully pay.
70. **COBRA Insurance** – Temporary continuation of employer health

insurance after a major life event.

71. **Charitable Giving** – Donating money or assets to a qualified non-profit or charity.
72. **Donor-Advised Fund (DAF)** – A charitable account allowing you to recommend grants over time.
73. **Qualified Charitable Distribution (QCD)** – A direct transfer from an IRA to charity, excluding it from taxable income.
74. **Appreciated Assets** – Investments or property that have increased in value.
75. **Capital Loss** – The loss incurred when selling an asset for less than its purchase price.
76. **Liquidity** – How easily an asset can be converted into cash.
77. **Diversification** – Spreading investments across different assets to reduce risk.
78. **Risk Tolerance** – Your ability and willingness to endure losses in investment value.
79. **Asset Allocation** – Dividing investments among different asset classes (stocks, bonds, cash).
80. **Mutual Fund** – A pool of money from many investors used to invest in securities.
81. **ETF (Exchange-Traded Fund)** – A fund that trades like a stock but holds a basket of investments.
82. **Index Fund** – A fund designed to track the performance of a market index.
83. **Dividend** – A portion of a company's earnings paid to shareholders.
84. **Bond** – A loan made to a corporation or government that pays interest over time.
85. **Stock** – A share representing ownership in a company.
86. **Real Estate Investment Trust (REIT)** – A company owning or financing real estate investments.
87. **401(k) Loan** – A loan taken against your 401(k) retirement account.
88. **Distribution** – Money taken out of a retirement account.
89. **Early Withdrawal Penalty** – A fee charged for taking money out of

retirement accounts before a certain age.

90. **Estate Planning** – Organizing the management and distribution of your assets after death.
91. **Durable Power of Attorney** – A power of attorney that remains in effect if you become incapacitated.
92. **Healthcare Proxy** – A person authorized to make medical decisions on your behalf.
93. **Living Will** – A document stating your medical treatment preferences if you can't communicate.
94. **Irrevocable Trust** – A trust that cannot be modified after creation without beneficiary consent.
95. **Revocable Trust** – A trust that can be changed or revoked by the grantor.
96. **Grantor** – The person who creates a trust.
97. **Trustee** – The person or institution responsible for managing trust assets.
98. **Guardian** – A person appointed to care for minor children if both parents die.
99. **Heir** – A person legally entitled to inherit part of an estate.
100. **Letter of Instruction** – A non-legal document giving guidance to heirs and executors about your final wishes.

Made in the USA
Monee, IL
12 February 2026

44022974R00203